Men

American Indies

Series Editors: Gary Needham and Yannis Tzioumakis

Titles in the series include:

The Spanish Prisoner
Yannis Tzioumakis
978 0 7486 3368 5 (hbk)
978 0 7486 3369 2 (pbk)

Lost in Translation
Geoff King
978 0 7486 3745 4 (hbk)
978 0 7486 3746 1 (pbk)

Memento
Claire Molloy
978 0 7486 3771 3 (hbk)
978 0 7486 3772 0 (pbk)

Brokeback Mountain
Gary Needham
978 0 7486 3382 1 (hbk)
978 0 7486 3383 8 (pbk)

Forthcoming titles include:

Far From Heaven
Glyn Davis
978 0 7486 3778 2 (hbk)
978 0 7486 3779 9 (pbk)

Memento

Claire Molloy

Edinburgh University Press

© Claire Molloy, 2010
Film stills © Newmarket / I Remember Productions

Edinburgh University Press Ltd
22 George Square, Edinburgh

www.euppublishing.com

Typeset in 11/13pt Monotype Baskerville by
Servis Filmsetting Ltd, Stockport, Cheshire, and
printed and bound by CPI Antony Rowe, Chippenham and Eastbourne

A CIP record for this book is available from the British Library

ISBN 978 0 7486 3771 3 (hardback)
ISBN 978 0 7486 3772 0 (paperback)

Contents

Series Preface

In recent years American independent cinema has not only become the focus of significant scholarly attention but as a category of film it has shifted from a marginal to a central position within American cinema – a shift that can also be detected in the emergence of the label indie cinema as opposed to independent cinema. The popularisation of this indie brand of filmmaking began in the 1990s with the commercial success of the Sundance Film Festival and of specialty distributor Miramax Films, as well as the introduction of DVD, which made independent films more readily available as well as profitable for the first time. At the same time, film studies started developing courses that distinguished American independent cinema from mainstream Hollywood, treating it as a separate object of study and a distinct discursive category.

Despite the surge in interest in independent cinema, a surge that involved the publication of at least twenty books and edited collections alongside a much larger number of articles on various aspects of independent cinema, especially about the post-1980 era, the field – as it has developed – still remains greatly under-researched in relation to the changes of the past twenty years that define the shift from independent to 'indie' cinema. This is partly because a multifaceted phenomenon such as American independent cinema, the history of which is as long and complex as the history of mainstream Hollywood, has yet to be adequately and satisfactorily documented. In this respect, academic film criticism is still in great need to account for the plethora of shapes, forms and guises that American independent cinema has manifested itself in. This is certainly not an easy task given that independent film has, indeed, taken a wide variety of forms at different historical trajectories and has been influenced by a hugely diverse range of factors.

It is with this problem in mind that 'American Indies' was conceived by its editors. While the history of American independent cinema is still being written with more studies already set to be published in future years, and while journal articles are enhancing our understanding of more focused aspects of independent filmmaking, the 'American Indies' series has been created to provide the necessary space to explore and engage with specific examples of American 'indie' films in a great depth. Through this format, 'American Indies' aims to encourage an examination of both the 'indie' text and its contexts, of understanding how 'indie' films operate within a particular filmmaking practice but also how 'indies' have been shaping a new formation of American cinema. In this respect, 'American Indies' provides the space for a detailed examination of industrial, economic and institutional concerns alongside the more usual formal and aesthetic considerations that have historically characterised critical approaches of independent films. 'American Indies' is a series of comprehensive studies of carefully selected examples of recent films that reveal in great detail the many sides of the phenomenon of the recently emerged American 'indie' cinema.

As the first book series to explore and define this aspect of American cinema, 'American Indies' has had the extremely difficult task of producing a comprehensive set of criteria that informs its selection of titles. Given the vastness of the field, we have made several editorial decisions in order to produce a coherent definition of this new phase of American independent cinema. The first such choice was to concentrate on recent examples of independent cinema. Although the word 'recent' has often been used to include films made in the post-1980 period, as editors we decided that the cut-off point for films to be included in this series would be the year 1996. This was an extremely significant year in the independent film sector, 'the year of the independents' as was triumphantly proclaimed by the *Los Angeles Business Journal* in February 1997, for a number of reasons. Arguably, the most significant of these reasons was the dynamic entrance in the film market of Fox Searchlight, a new type of a specialty film division created by Twentieth Century Fox in 1995 with the explicit intention of claiming a piece of the increasingly large independent film market pie. Fox Searchlight would achieve this objective through the production and distribution of films that followed many of the conventions of independent film as those were established after the success of *sex, lies and videotape* in 1989. These conventions had since then started being popularised by a number of films produced and distributed by Miramax Films, an independent company that was taken over by Disney after the phenomenal box office success of several of its films at approximately the same time as Twentieth Century Fox was establishing its specialty division.

The now direct involvement of entertainment conglomerates like Disney and Fox in the independent film sector had far-reaching effects. Arguably, the most important of these was that the label 'independent', which for critics and the cinema going public (wrongly) signified economic independence from major film companies like Disney, Fox, Paramount, Universal, etc., obviously ceased to convey this meaning. Instead, critics and public alike increasingly started using the label 'indie', which suggested a particular type of film that adhered to a set of conventions as well as a transformed independent cinema sector that was now driven by specialty companies, most of which subsidiaries of major entertainment conglomerates. It is this form of 'independent' cinema that has produced some of the most interesting films to come out from American cinema in recent years that 'American Indies' has set out to explore in great depth and which explains our selection of the label 'indies' instead of independents.

We hope readers will enjoy the series

Gary Needham and Yannis Tzioumakis
American Indies Series Editors

Acknowledgements

My sincere thanks go to the series editors, Gary Needham and Yannis Tzioumakis, for choosing to include this book in the American Indies series. I am extremely grateful to Gary for his ongoing support and his constructive and insightful comments which were so beneficial to me, particularly in the later stages of writing. My heartfelt thanks go to Yannis for being a thoroughly supportive and extremely knowledgeable editor, an expert guide throughout every aspect of this project as well as being a truly great and valued mentor, friend, colleague and scholar.

I received funding for research and study leave from Liverpool John Moores University which enabled me to complete the final section of this book and for which I am most grateful. Thanks to my colleagues at John Moores University, particularly those who offered feedback on an early draft chapter, and those who gave help and support along the way. I must also acknowledge the kind assistance given to me by staff at the Margaret Herrick Library during my visit to Los Angeles to gather research materials.

I have received endless support from my wonderful family and would like to thank my parents, Nina and Christopher Parkinson, and my brother, Richard, for all they have done and continue to do for me. Finally, thanks to my partner, Andy, who has encouraged me, at times acted as a research assistant, talked through aspects of the book and has had endless patience with me during the research and writing. For these reasons and many more I am forever grateful to him.

For 'Danny' – always in my memories.

Introduction: *Memento*

Memento emerged into the new landscape of twenty-first-century independent film. As the dust settled on the twentieth century, the corporate
and independent sectors had blurred into new entities which raised questions about what independent film had become. On one level *Memento*
sat comfortably within one definition of late twentieth-century independence. Produced and distributed by Newmarket, in financial terms the
film occupied the low-budget end of the production spectrum with an
initial cost of $5 million.[1] In formal terms *Memento*'s innovative and chal-
lenging narrative structure added to its independent credentials, fitting
the mould of the off-beat film which would never have been made in a
Hollywood system that shied away from such narrative experimentation. At the Sundance Film Festival in 2001, however, critics questioned
the film's independence, pointing out that the producers, Jennifer Todd
and Suzanne Todd, had a commercial pedigree garnered from films
such as *Austin Powers: International Man of Mystery* (Roach, 1997), *Austin
Powers: The Spy Who Shagged Me* (Roach, 1999) and *G.I. Jane* (Scott, 1997).[2]
Elsewhere the independent sensibility of *Memento* was challenged, with
the film described as being oriented towards a mass commercial audience.[3] In this sense, 'independence' was compromised by an association
with the mainstream and questions about *Memento*'s 'indie' qualifications
served to illustrate the complex and contentious terrain of contemporary
American independent cinema.

   This book is centrally concerned with placing *Memento* within that
terrain constituted of the various discourses which construct independence. In the process it examines the context of the film's production, the
practices used in its marketing and distribution, its negotiation of narrative norms and its public reception. In each of these aspects *Memento* has
something to say about independent film, yet the construction of meanings about independence is not straightforward. Instead, independence

operates within a set of discourses that are constantly in flux. These discourses are shaped by various interests that are in turn contingent on each other for constructing their own definitions and discursive boundaries. In this way, for instance, within particular discourses the production of knowledge and construction of meanings about commercial mainstream cinema is crucial to the establishment and maintenance of meanings about independent cinema; one is invoked to make sense of the other. But this is not to propose that a discourse of independence is produced from an overarching oppositional mainstream–independent binary; this would require fixed authorities of delimitation and stable lines of difference. Instead, there is always a multiplicity of discourses in circulation which serve many different interests, and, in the case of independent film, include those of producers, distributors, fans, cinephiles, critics, academics and many more besides. As the interests of groups shift and change, discourses will necessarily be established, adapted, negotiated and revised.[4]

Such a position draws on an understanding of discourse as proposed by Michel Foucault, rather than as a more general linguistic concept. In the Foucauldian sense, discourses are the manifestations of what can legitimately be said about a particular topic within different historical periods. However, discourses delimit and define acceptable practices, ideas and ways of talking, and therefore also regulate or restrict other statements about a topic. Although an object of discourse is identified and defined by an authority, discourses are not closed, but instead are subject to change over time giving rise to multiple and competing 'truths'. In other words, practices, objects of study and forms of knowledge are connected through discursive formations to the extent that within an historical period different forms of knowledge production and authorities give rise to 'independence' as an object of multiple discourses. Discourses of independence are therefore historically specific and unfixed, and describe relations of power.

This multiplicity of discourses has been evident in the ongoing struggle to reach a consensus on what independent film means, and was amply demonstrated in a 1996 edition of the magazine *Filmmaker*, which asked producers, distributors, critics and curators to identify the most important American independent films of all time.[5] Reporting that respondents had been confused by the term 'independent' and that some had 'brought up the age-old question of what constitutes an independent film', the article stated that the magazine had been purposefully vague as it 'wanted the responses to define "independent" film'.[6] As the range of films offered by the respondents included the 1948 *noir Force of Evil* (Polonsky, 1948), Charlie Chaplin's *City Lights* (1931), Robert Flaherty's *Nanook of the North* (1922), Nicolas Ray's western *Johnny Guitar* (1954), Jean-Luc Godard's *Breathless* [*Àbout de soufflé*] (1960) and Chris Marker's *La Jetée* [*The Pier*] (1962) this did little to clarify the nebulous terminology. Moreover, the films that the respondents suggested, such as *Breathless* which was at the top of James Schamus's Top 50 list, complicated any concrete definitions of what constituted American film, a point conceded by *Filmmaker*, which noted that 'for some, "American independent" was not limited by geography' and that *Breathless* and *La Jetée* were deemed to be 'vital to the consciousness of indie filmmakers'.[7] In the final list *Filmmaker* gave *sex, lies and videotape* (Soderbergh, 1989), a film considered in other accounts to mark the beginning of the contemporary era of independent film, fourth place behind *Stranger than Paradise* (Jarmusch, 1984), *She's Gotta Have It* (Lee, 1986) and, in first place, *A Woman Under the Influence* (1974), describing Cassavetes as 'the quintessential American indie'.[8] Completing the top ten films in the list were, in fifth place, John Sayles' (1980) *Return of the Secaucus Seven*, followed by *Harlan County, USA* (Kopple, 1976), *The Thin Blue Line* (Morris, 1986), *Scorpio Rising* (Anger, 1964), *Blood Simple* (Coen, 1984) and finally, Richard Linklater's (1991) *Slacker*.

The *Fimmaker* Top 50 draws attention to the contested nature of independence within different authoritative groups. Despite having shared interests in independent film and having some coherence as groups with affiliations to *Filmmaker*, differences of opinion had to be negotiated to produce a top 50 independent canon. Bounded by a different set of limits more than a decade later, the film magazine *Empire* applied criteria to rank the Top Fifty Greatest Independent Films which '[took] into account the quality of the film, the circumstances behind its production, the achievement of the filmmakers despite monetary and logistical constraints and its influence on subsequent projects'.[9] With *Memento* listed at number thirteen, the top ten films in the *Empire* list have only one in common with the 1996 *Filmmaker* line-up – *sex, lies and videotape* comes seventh place. The top five places in *Empire*'s list are *Monty Python's Life of Brian* (Jones, 1979), *Clerks* (Smith, 1994), *The Terminator* (Cameron, 1984), *Donnie Darko* (Kelly, 2001) and, in top spot, *Reservoir Dogs* (Tarantino, 1992).[10] A further indie corpus is produced by The Internet Movie Database (IMDb) Top Rated 'Independent' Films, which places *Memento* in sixth position and has *Pulp Fiction* (Tarantino, 1994) claiming first place as rated by registered users of IMDb.[11] What these three canons demonstrate is that independence has different meanings for different groups at different times. In other words, authorities set various limits on discourses of independence, distinct rules and practices by which 'independent' is constructed and classified. For instance, *Empire* claimed: 'Bearing in mind that to encompass all those that are independently financed would mean *The Phantom Menace* is an independent film we've qualified all entries by ensuring they were made with what *we* consider to be an independent spirit' (emphasis added).[12] In producing a 'top 50 list', each of the authorities concerned – producers, distributors, critics and curators in the case of *Filmmaker*, film journalists and critics at *Empire*, and an online public community in the case of IMDb – are also involved in the production, normalisation and exclusion of particular tastes, values and definitions. Conceived in this way, each canon has resonance for social groups and identities whereby individuals can locate themselves within discourses, making sense of their own practices of consumption and taste preferences. These discourses are thus also relational and contingent, their meanings constructed through understandings of what independence is not as much as what it is at any given moment.

In terms of historicising discursive activity, the 1990s was a period of acceleration in the multiplication of discourses of independence, facilitated by wider social, economic, political and cultural changes. The loosening of international economic policies and expansion of media markets led to changes in the availability of money for independent production with international finance supporting a growing sector. There was a rapid rise in the number of channels carrying cultural content, as well as the expansion and availability of international markets which independent film was able to exploit. Sector changes were brisk, with increases in the amount of activity in relation to the acquisition and purchase of companies. Alongside this, consumption practices changed with the destabilisation and fragmentation of mass identities as consumption became recognised as intrinsically tied to the creation and maintenance of self-identity. Niche media acknowledged this fragmentation, targeting evermore focused consumer identities and giving independent film an array of cost-effective routes to reach its audience. Changes in technologies reshaped producer–consumer relations, opened up new marketing possibilities for indie films and, in terms of camera, post-production and exhibition technologies, gave a greater range of choices to independent filmmakers and distributors. As such, the rapidity of these changes was accompanied by a parallel proliferation of discourses of independence.

This account inevitably sweeps a broad and rather crude brush across what are highly complex and important changes which can better be described by recourse to theories of globalisation, poststructuralism and postmodernism, but the point here is to establish that independent cinema is not independent of any of these contexts. These were the social, cultural and economic conditions within which *Memento* was produced, distributed and consumed, thus the film offers a route to thinking about the ways in which these forces shaped late American independent cinema. *Memento* is a product of these changes and shifts inasmuch as it offers a deliberation on them.

It is worth acknowledging, of course, that *Memento* is a significant film for many reasons, not least because it was the film that brought director/writer Christopher Nolan to the attention of studios, critics and the public. In reviews of his later films, including Warner Bros'. blockbuster *The Dark Knight* (Nolan, 2008), *Memento* continues to be mentioned, and in many cases is considered as a defining film in the Nolan 'canon'. A typical review of *The Dark Knight* in *Variety* made the comparison: 'Though more linear than "*Memento*" and "*The Prestige*" . . . "*The Dark Knight*" pivots with similar ingenuity on a breathless series of twists and turns . . .' and elsewhere, 'Christopher Nolan used the unique storytelling that made *Memento* so bracing to revive the *Batman* franchise for Warner Bros'.[13] *Memento* has been crucial to defining Nolan's status as an independent director, an identity that he has continued to foster, claiming in an interview in 2006: 'I feel like an indie filmmaker working inside the studio system' and articulating the requirement for independence within studio filmmaking: 'I approached them with the idea. They already knew that studio filmmaking had screwed up this franchise. They couldn't do it their way, so I got to do it my way.'[14] In a later *Variety* article entitled 'Nolan Brings Indie Sensibility to Knight', the 'indie sensibility' to which the title refers develops this discourse of independence and positions the director as an *auteur* involved in 'serious filmmaking', able to apply the 'same meticulously detailed and deeply thought-out psychological approach to the material as in his earlier, low-budget efforts'.[15] In this sense, *Memento* has been absolutely central to maintaining Nolan's identity as an 'indie' director and has functioned, retrospectively, as a prominent exemplar of independent filmmaking. Moreover, claims that an independent sensibility can be brought to a studio blockbuster such as *The Dark Knight* also imply that 'indie' can be both co-opted and commercially marketable, and furthermore that *Memento* continues to be an important element within that marketing discourse.[16]

Memento was also an immensely important film for Newmarket Entertainment Group as Newmarket Films was created specifically to distribute the film, a move that expanded the interests of the company beyond production financing. As such the film was crucial to the changes in Newmarket's organisation and fortunes. In financial terms, *Memento* was the 'indie' hit of 2001 and in terms of its reception the film received widespread critical acclaim and garnered numerous critics' and festival awards, including the Waldo Salt Screenwriting Award at the Sundance Film Festival and Best Director, Best Feature, Best Screenplay and Best Supporting Female awards at the Independent Spirit Awards in 2002. In addition, the film's innovative narrative structure has fascinated critics, academics and fans and the film continues to generate much discussion and critical debate, particularly on the issues of identity, memory, time, agency and truth.

Each of these points underlines *Memento*'s status as a film worthy of study in its own right and the aim of the chapters that follow is to contextualise these matters within debates about independent cinema. To these ends, chapter 1 offers a history of Newmarket and situates the company within the changing economics of the independent sector since the 1990s.[17]Newmarket was involved in production financing for a range of independent and studio films prior to *Memento* and also diversified into home entertainment distribution before moving into theatrical distribution with a one-film slate in 2001. Chapter 1 also offers an account of some of the ways in which American independent cinema has been dependent on external economics and markets, and then explores these issues in relation to *Memento*. Specifically, it looks at how European distribution deals financed the film's production and how a controlling interest in Newmarket was acquired by the German media company Helkon. Chapter 2 looks towards independent marketing strategies to propose that, once it had reached maturation, the independent apparatus co-opted mainstream media forms, particularly through the production of narratives about independent filmmakers that were necessarily reductive. Independent and indie emerged as marketable categories and Chapter 2 examines aspects of *Memento*'s marketing in both the US and UK to ascertain what signifiers of independence were utilised, particularly in early print advertisements.

Chapter 3 focuses on narrative and offers a scene-by-scene analysis of *Memento* with the aim of identifying how the film creates and maintains ambiguity. This analysis is considered within the context of new forms of reception and the wider shift towards complex narratives to explore how *Memento* has consciously exploited the possibilities of DVD and the trend for multiple viewings of a single film. Chapter 4 is concerned with *film noir* and an analysis of gender difference within *Memento* to reveal the extent to which notions of disability problematise constructions of masculinity. Finally, much of *Memento*'s word of mouth was generated online and chapter 5 examines the public discourse on the film and explores how this developed within Internet communities. The final chapter also returns to the issue of categorising *Memento* as an independent film and explores the extent to which its independent status figured in its public reception and eventual success.

Memento is a film that defies easy comprehension and continues to be regarded by many as an example of independent creativity and innovation. It is a film for which many critics and scholars – myself included – confess to having, what Henry Jenkins would refer to as a 'fannish enthusiasm'.[18] Suffice to say, *Memento* is, without doubt, hugely significant within the corpus of twenty-first-century independent films.

1 *Memento* and Independent Cinema: A Seductive Business

'We're financiers, not movie people.'

'It's a seductive business, but we're certainly not seduced by it.'

William Tyrer and Christopher Ball, co-founders of Newmarket Group[1]

By the time *Memento* reached Sundance in 2001, a series of corporate takeovers and mergers, which had started in the early 1990s, notably including New Line Cinema and Miramax in 1993, had dramatically reshaped the independent sector. New Line Cinema had been established in 1967 as an independent non-theatrical distributor until, in 1973, the company moved into the distribution of exploitation and art movies. Targeting the markets that the majors ignored, New Line's roster included George Romero's *Night of the Living Dead* (1968), Jean-Luc Godard's *Sympathy for the Devil* (1968), John Waters' *Pink Flamingos* (1972) and Hooper's *The Texas Chainsaw Massacre* (1974). In the early1980s New Line found commercial success with the *Nightmare on Elm Street* franchise. The first film in the series, directed by Wes Craven in 1984 with a budget of less than $2 million, took more than $10 million at the domestic box office and the next three *Nightmare on Elm Street* films continued to record healthy box office grosses of $23 million, $44 million and $45 million respectively.[2] New Line was able to follow this success with a second franchise and, in the 1990s, the first of four films in the *Teenage Mutant Ninja Turtles* series took over $135 million at the domestic box office. This success attracted the attention of Ted Turner, and New Line was bought in 1993 by Turner Broadcasting System which then merged with Time Warner in 1996.

Another key catalyst to change in the sector was independent distributor Miramax, established by Harvey and Bob Weinstein in 1979 and acquired by Disney in 1993. Miramax redefined what was possible in terms of independent success with films such as *sex, lies and videotape*, which grossed $24.7 million, and *The Crying Game* (Jordan, 1992), which realised $62.5 million. Miramax demonstrated that there was a new market for low-budget independent film and, significantly, showed that a company name could function as a brand label with cinema-going audiences. One of the company's strengths lay in its aggressive marketing which, in the case of *sex, lies and videotape*, borrowed much from exploitation strategies to bolster the film's commercial appeal.[3] For *The Crying Game* Miramax used a 'don't-reveal-the-secret strategy', which proved extremely successful with critics, audiences and the popular media.[4] *Time Magazine*, for instance, ran an article with the headline 'Don't Read This Story' which explained:

We're about to reveal a secret of *The Crying Game*, and we don't want to spoil the pleasure of the uninitiated. So you who have not seen this film, turn the page, or tear it out and save it to consult later. Any cheating will be punished. No kidding. We have ways.[5]

Other aspects of Miramax's innovative approach to marketing included the adoption of genre film release patterns for art-house films, the use of television advertising and, significantly, the company took full advantage of a film's critical acclaim by foregrounding awards in advertising campaigns.[6] Combined with the controversial publicity that the company courted, these strategies paid off and led to crossover successes for individual films and to wider audience recognition of the Miramax brand.[7] In the case of *Pulp Fiction*, the first of its films to gross in excess of $100 million, the company was able through its marketing strategies to exploit the film's commercial and art-house potential and, in doing so, succeeded with what Peter Biskind refers to as an 'art film . . . for the multiplex audience'.[8]

The independent sector enjoyed a period of expansion during the 1990s and benefited from an economic upturn as major international financial institutions looked to film financing as a high-yield business.[9] The successes of films such as *sex, lies and videotape* and *Sling Blade* (Thornton, 1996), each made for under $2 million and grossing over $24 million, suggested that independent film could offer large returns for a relatively small initial investment. Another key element in the growth of the sector was the development of European television markets which gave American independent film an important avenue for financing through foreign pre-sales of the distribution rights. These agreements were vital to funding as they allowed producers to approach the banks for money to cover the costs of production against the guaranteed foreign pre-sales. A further factor in the development of the sector in this period was the brief stabilisation of the completion bond business which provided insurances to banks offering production cost financing. In the early 1990s bond companies had been involved in a price-cutting war until a handful of bonded films, which included *The Adventures of Baron Munchausen* (Gilliam, 1988), *Hoffa* (DeVito, 1992), and *Malcolm X* (Lee, 1992), went disastrously over budget and drove the two main bonders, Film Finances and Completion Bond, to the brink of financial collapse.[10] Bonding was, however, increasingly important to the independent sector, with *Variety* reporting in 1997 that 'most independent films need a bond to get off the ground', and so renewed stability in the bonding business by the middle of the decade further enhanced the financial climate for independent film.[11]

Indicative of the growing number of independent films being made were the relative increases in festival submissions. In a ten-year period, submissions of dramatic features to the Sundance Film Festival rocketed from 60 in 1987 to over 800 in 1997.[12] To cater for films that failed to get a place at Sundance, Slamdance was established in 1995 and by 1996 submissions numbered 450. In 1997 this increased to over 1,000 and in 1998 and 1999 there were in excess of 1,300 and 1,700 submissions, respectively.[13] As Miramax was able to demonstrate to great effect, festival success could figure in the marketability and success of independent films. As well as festivals, awards and particularly the more 'glamorous' of the Academy Award nominations such as Best Picture, Best Actor and Best Actress also had the potential to boost a film's revenue at the box office.[14] *The Crying Game*, for instance, grossed $14 million at the domestic box office prior to the 1993 Academy Award nominations, $33.6 million following the nomination for Best Picture and $14.9 million following the Awards, giving the film 53.7 per cent of its total gross in the period between nominations and the Academy Awards.[15] Oscar success for the sector continued during the 1990s as independent films achieved new levels of popular and critical recognition. Throughout the decade the number of independently distributed films which featured in the Academy Award nominations became substantial. For instance, at the 1993 Academy Awards, New Line had two nominations – for *Glengarry Glen Ross* (Foley, 1992) and for *Damage* (Malle, 1992) – and Miramax received twelve nominations – six for *The Crying Game*, three for *Enchanted April* (Newell, 1992), two for *Passion Fish* (Sayles, 1992) and one for *Urga* (re-titled for the US market *Close To Eden* [Mikhalkov, 1991]). *Pulp Fiction* received seven nominations at the 1995 Awards whilst twenty-four of the remaining nominations that year were shared among twelve other independent productions which included, for Miramax, two nominations for *Tom & Viv* (Gilbert, 1994), one nomination for *Heavenly Creatures* (Jackson, 1994) and seven nominations for *Bullets Over Broadway* (Allen, 1994).

Influenced by the enormous success of New Line and in particular Miramax in terms of both box office and critical acclaim, the other major studios shifted their attention in an attempt to take a share of the independent market. In the six years following the New Line and Miramax acquisitions Twentieth-Century-Fox, Paramount, Sony and MGM also established specialty divisions (Fox Searchlight in 1994, Paramount Classics in 1998, Screen Gems in 1999 and United Artists Films in 1999, respectively) as independent arms of the corporate parent company charged to produce and/or distribute films characterised financially and/or aesthetically as something other than mainstream commercial studio offerings. What this all meant in real terms, however, varied from one specialty division to the next, as did the degree of independence that each enjoyed. Miramax retained a strategic and well-publicised distance from Disney with a contractual agreement that gave Harvey and Bob Weinstein total freedom, with any project capped under $12.5 million.[16] Their autonomy was tested early in the relationship, however, when Disney refused to let the company release Larry Clark's controversial début feature *Kids* (Clark, 1995), forcing the Weinstein brothers to set up a sub-distributor, Shining Excalibur Films, for the specific purpose of distributing the film.[17] The controversy underlined the problems associated with the blurring of boundaries between corporate and independent sectors and demonstrated that the studio-owned 'indie' labels always remained, at some level, accountable to their corporate 'parent'.

With the majors' move into the indie market, and with funding for production costs becoming relatively easy to acquire, there was an explosion in the sector which eventually led to a problem with overproduction which the market could not sustain. By the early 2000s, in an environment where the competition for North American distribution was particularly fierce, US distributors were criticised for being more interested in finding the next indie blockbuster than in pursuing 'niche' films. Miramax in particular was cited as problematic for competition in the sector by driving up the costs of acquisitions and pricing competitors out of the market.[18] At the same time, a more cautious international market had created a situation where foreign sales were increasingly dependent on films first having a US theatrical release. For this reason, a two-tier pricing system emerged, with international distributors paying a higher price for a film with North American distribution. However, if a film failed at the domestic box office its ancillary market price was dramatically reduced and it lost its value as a video and television commodity. For films without theatrical distribution there was the opportunity to get picked up by one of the growing number of cable-based US pay television services such as Viacom's Showtime Networks, HBO Networks and Liberty Media's Starz Encore, or to get a straight-to-video release. However, the abundance of indie product meant that even for those films which had distribution, there was intense competition for an audience and for securing release dates.

Overproduction was only one of the problems independent film was facing at the close of the 1990s and early 2000s. Diminishing foreign pre-sales to European television was equally important as these had weakened substantially following the boom years of the 1990s. The reason for this was the intensified competition in European countries' cable and satellite television sectors which had forced pay TV rates to plummet. After a period of rapid expansion in television services, European broadcasters found that, as more choice for the television consumer diluted audience share, it was predominantly blockbusters that delivered high ratings.[19] One consequence was that independent films struggled to get picked up by foreign distributors. In addition, there were serious problems with financing. When the independent sector had demonstrated strong growth competition had been created among banks, which were willing to lend against production cost budgets. Such were the levels of competition that loans often reached up to 40–50 per cent of a production budget. However, as the economic stability that the independent sector had enjoyed in the mid-1990s began to weaken and the pre-sales market evaporated, many producers could not meet the large loan commitments, defaulted on payments and were forced to surrender copyrights. The extent of the problem was apparent in the early 2000s when, for instance, Comerica's Entertainment Group declared $12 million of defaulted 'indie' loans in one quarter alone.[20]

Further problems, which were not unique to the independents but were felt across the entertainment and media industries, were linked to the loss of German investment and buyers, especially following the collapse of the Neuer Markt. After a period of aggressive investment and acquisition by German media companies of US film and media interests the slowdown and eventual crash of the German economy in 2000 and 2001 affected the American film industry substantially in terms of both direct investment and the loss of a key sales territory. By 2001 Helkon, Kirschgroup and Kinowelt Medien had filed for insolvency and with so many of the large media companies bankrupt and no longer buying US product, Germany ceased to be a viable sales territory. As it had been a major substantial buyer of independent films the loss of this territory's film sales was a blow not only to the independent sector but to the industry as a whole. It is within this rapidly expanding and changing independent sector that Newmarket was established.

Newmarket Capital Group

Newmarket Capital Group was established in 1994 by two British expatriates, William A. Tyrer and Christopher Ball. Both men were experienced entertainment financiers and, from 1989, worked together as executives at the Los Angeles office of Lloyds Bank where they were involved in financing against film pre-sales. In 1990 the Japanese-owned Daiwa Bank purchased a number of Lloyds' American commercial banking interests, including Lloyds Bank LA, and Tyrer and Ball moved the film finance business into Daiwa's commercial banking division. The same year Daiwa financed *Hamlet* (Zefirelli, 1990), the first film for Mel Gibson's production company, Icon. This established the relationship between Tyrer, Ball and Gibson's Icon Entertainment International, a partnership that would find phenomenal success fourteen years later, in 2004, when Newmarket distributed *The Passion of the Christ* (Gibson, 2004). If Miramax had redefined the commercial potential of independent film with the indie blockbuster *Pulp Fiction* in the 1990s then Newmarket rewrote what was possible for an independent venture in the 2000s when *The Passion of the Christ* grossed over $600 million worldwide.[21] Over the decade between the establishment of the Newmarket Capital Group and the success with *Passion* in 2004, the company moved from its earlier incarnation as a boutique financier to expansion into acquisitions, production and distribution. The main shift in the company's direction into theatrical distribution occurred in 2000 with *Memento*.

With capital provided by Farallon Capital Management and investment from a hedge fund, Newmarket's business model in 1994 anticipated a later, large-scale move by Hollywood and the independent sector towards hedge fund film financing in the 2000s.[22] The initial intention was that Newmarket would be able to offer finance of between $3 million and $40 million as collateralised loans or partial and complete funding to producers before the foreign pre-sales for a film were finalised.[23] This was a more flexible approach to financing than that offered by the commercial banks, which would only agree loans for financing on the basis of guaranteed foreign pre-sales. Newmarket was therefore in a position to begin funding at an earlier stage in the process and offered larger gap coverage.[24] Another attraction of Newmarket for independent producers of mid-budget productions was that Tyrer and Ball were able to give the go-ahead to projects up to $10 million which avoided the complexities of independents having to find financing from multiple sources.[25]

Two of the first ventures for the newly established Newmarket were involvement in the production financing of *The Usual Suspects* (Singer, 1995) and *Dead Man* (Jarmusch, 1995). *The Usual Suspects*, shot in thirty-five days for $5.5 million and distributed by Gramercy, grossed $23 million and won two Academy Awards: Best Actor in a Supporting Role for Kevin Spacey, and Best Screenplay Written Directly for the Screen for Christopher McQuarrie. Jim Jarmusch's *Dead Man* achieved critical acclaim, was nominated for a Golden Palm at Cannes Film Festival, won the 1996 New York Film Critics Circle Best Cinematographer award for Robby Müller (which it shared with *Breaking the Waves* [Von Trier, 1996]) and the 1996 Felix's Screen International Five Continents Award for Best Non-European Film. In terms of domestic box office, however, *Dead Man*, distributed by Miramax, did not fare well despite being directed by Jim Jarmusch, and took just over $1 million against a budget of $9 million.[26] Newmarket's early projects, one a commercial success and the other a critical success, illustrated particularly well the diverse range of films that the company would continue to foster.

In 1995 Newmarket was able to secure a $15 million line of credit from the Bank of America, which allowed the company the option to invest in projects that exceeded their original $40 million ceiling. In 1998 the company received a further $30 million credit facility from Union Bank. With pressure for pre-sellable elements, such as a marketable director or cast to guarantee overseas pre-sales, the market for low-budget productions of between $3 and $5 million started to falter in the mid-1990s. Newmarket's strategy was to turn to the gap in the market for mid-budget projects of between $10 and $20 million, notably providing the total $11 million of finance for Original Films' *Cruel Intentions*

(Kumble, 1999), starring Sarah Michelle Geller and Reese Witherspoon and produced by Neal Moritz.

Newmarket signed what was initially a four-year deal for $100 million of capital with Moritz's Original Films company to produce and finance a slate of genre pictures which eventually included *Skulls* (Cohen 2000), *Cruel Intentions II* (Kumble, 2000), *The Skulls II* (Chappelle, 2002), *The Skulls III* (Dale, 2003), *Cruel Intentions III* (Ziehl, 2004) and *Prom Night* (McCormick, 2008). Original Films had a first-look deal in place with Columbia, which subsequently handled the distribution for the *Cruel Intentions* series. *Intentions* grossed $38 million against an $11 million budget, whilst *Cruel Intentions II* and *III* were straight-to-video releases through Columbia TriStar Home Video. The *Skulls* trilogy followed a similar strategy, with a theatrical release only for the first film in the series, which was distributed by Universal eager to exploit the lucrative teen market and with foreign sales handled by Summit. *The Skulls* grossed $35 million against a budget of $15 million. For Original and Newmarket the aim was to target specific segments of the audience with very commercial, smaller-budget genre films and to find foreign distribution partners in overseas territories.

As well as the Original Films deal, in 1998 Newmarket also entered into an agreement with Mutual Film Company to finance several mid-budget pictures in the $8–15 million range. Newmarket had already worked with Mutual and had been involved in the financing of two projects for the company: *A Simple Plan* (Raimi, 1998), produced by Paramount, which garnered numerous awards and critical praise for Billy Bob Thornton's supporting role as Jacob Mitchell, but grossed only $16 million against a budget of $17 million; and *Hard Rain* (Salomon, 1998) with a production budget of $70 million and a strong cast – Morgan Freeman, Christian Slater, Randy Quaid and Minnie Driver – but which took only $19.8 million at the domestic box office. Other relationships established during the first four years of Newmarket's operations included those with Good Machine International, Icon, CiBy and Summit and a widely reported pact with Buena Vista Film Sales and John Woo and Terence Chang's Lion Rock Productions to finance a string of under $20 million action movies. From these ventures came *The King Is Alive* (Levring, 2000), co-produced and distributed with Good Machine International, Icon Entertainment International's *Felicia's Journey* (Egoyan, 1999), *Velvet Goldmine* (Haynes, 1998), produced by Miramax and distributed by CiBy Sales, and *The Loss of Sexual Innocence*

(Figgis, 1999), co-produced with Summit. Newmarket and Summit also bought rights in all non-English-speaking territories to the hugely successful *American Pie* (Weitz, 1999), which was distributed in the US, UK, Canada, Australia, New Zealand and South Africa by Universal. *American Pie* grossed $102 million domestic and $235 worldwide, against a production budget of just $11 million.

The Summit relationship was important for Newmarket as the company had a strong profile as an independent international sales company. Summit, controlled by Patrick Wachsberger but started in 1991 by producers Arnon Milchan, Andrew Vajna and Bernd Eichinger, expanded into production and co-financing in 1995 and finally into fully financing productions in 1997 with Mike Figgis' *The Loss of Sexual Innocence*. Summit's shift in direction was indicative of changes in the marketplace as its relationships with Cinergi Pictures Entertainment and Mandalay Entertainment had ended when Cinergi went out of business and Mandalay choose Sony Pictures Entertainment to handle its foreign sales. After a failed attempt to handle sales for films generated through the UK Lottery consortium, Summit was obliged to increase its in-house production. The next year, a deal between Summit and Artisan Entertainment created what one trade paper referred to as 'the world's first super-indie' and 'the largest independent entity outside the studio system'.[27] The alliance brought together Artisan – a domestic distributor with a substantial library in excess of 2,000 titles which included *Reservoir Dogs* (Tarantino, 1992), *Terminator 2: Judgment Day* (Cameron, 1991), *Dirty Dancing* (Ardolino, 1987), *Total Recall* (Verhoeven, 1990) and the *Rambo* series – and Summit, with its expertise in international sales.

In partnership with Summit in 1998, Newmarket began to develop *The Mexican* (Verbinski, 2001) from a script written by J. H. Wyman with the intention of financing the project at around $8–10 million. Hoping to expand their network of relationships with commercially successful producers, Newmarket brought Lawrence Bender in to produce. Bender had an impressive record having already produced *Good Will Hunting* (Van Sant, 1997) as well as working with director Quentin Tarantino as the producer on *Reservoir Dogs* (1992), *Pulp Fiction* (1994), *Four Rooms* (Anders, Rockwell, Rodriguez and Tarantino, 1995) and *Jackie Brown* (1997). Initially *The Mexican* was to be directed by David Fincher with Brad Pitt in the lead role, but Fincher withdrew from the project, which was subsequently picked up by Jeffrey Katzenberg at Dreamworks SKG. Gore Verbinski succeeded Fincher as director and Katzenberg brought

Julia Roberts in to play the role of Samantha Barzel. With a star cast, the budget went from a $10 million indie production to a $57 million studio project. *The Mexican* grossed $66 million at the domestic box office and $147 million worldwide and put Newmarket 'officially on the Hollywood radar'.[28]

By 1999 Newmarket had been involved with a cluster of successful films for the teen market (*Cruel Intentions*, *Skulls* and *American Pie*) as well as independent projects that included *Splendor* (Araki, 1999) *Rogue Trader* (Dearden, 1999), *Twelfth Night* (Nunn, 1996), *Mrs Dalloway* (Gorris, 1997) and *Roseanna's Grave* (Weiland, 1997). It also had an involvement with Andy and Larry Wachowski's *Bound* (1996), Todd Haynes' *Velvet Goldmine*, Kristian Levring's *The King Is Alive* (produced under the Dogme banner) and Niki Caro's *Memory and Desire* (1997). Whilst the projects were varied and included financing for studio and independent films, the common theme for many of the company's ventures was the $10–20 million range. Given the market at that time, Newmarket's plan to finance mid-budget productions, establish good relationships with commercially successful producers and sales agents and finance, some 15–20 projects a year proved to be a viable strategy. Mid-budget films did flourish during the 1990s and many sub-$20 million films achieved good box office profits as well as critical recognition. For instance, at the 1998 Academy Awards *Good Will Hunting* (Van Sant, 1997) with a budget of $10 million was nominated for nine awards and grossed $138 million; *Boogie Nights* (Anderson, 1997) had a budget of $15 million, received three nominations and grossed $26 million; and *Wag The Dog* (Levinson, 1997) had a budget of $15 million, received two nominations and grossed $43 million.

In 1999 Newmarket diversified with the establishment of a home entertainment distribution arm, Saturn Home Entertainment. Although the video rental market was faltering at this time, the DVD market was emerging and with the availability of a large number of independent titles thanks to overproduction in the sector, Newmarket was able to capitalise on the home entertainment business for non-theatrical films.[29] The new distribution arm was headed by the former president of Lions Gate Home Entertainment, Barry Brooker, with the intention of acquiring television rights and producing as well as acquiring and licensing straight-to-video titles. Saturn Home Entertainment was kept quite separate from the theatrical end of Newmarket's business and reflected the changing home entertainment market with releases comprised of

80 per cent VHS and 20 per cent DVD in the first year of operation. The success of Saturn Home Entertainment was apparent when, in an interview in May 2000, William Tyrer noted that Newmarket's home video and DVD distribution company would 'keep profits up even if Newmarket didn't produce a movie all year'.[30]

In the last quarter of 1999 Newmarket went into negotiations with German production and distribution company Helkon Media to finance productions with a $100 million line of credit. The Helkon – Newmarket pact was one of a number of German – North American agreements taking place at the time with an influx of German money into various US operations which included a $10.5 million investment by Tele-Munchen in Lions Gate Entertainment and acquisitions by German distributors Splendid Films and Kinowelt Medien of stakes in Initial Entertainment and Alliance Atlantis, respectively. Helkon had been founded in 1991 by Werner Koenig and Martin Heldmann as a German TV licensing company but quickly moved into production and theatrical distribution. By 1996 the company was reported to hold the rights to 300 films which it used as collateral to build up a credit line. Having agreements with Seven Arts, Ed Pressman, Dark Castle, Buena Vista and Intermedia, Helkon went public on the Neuer Markt in 1999 and, along with the purchase of an initial 19 per cent share in Newmarket in 2000, Koenig and Haldmann's company also bought a 51 per cent share in the UK film distributor Redbus Film Distribution. Helkon bought a further 32 per cent interest in Newmarket in mid-2000 to bring its share to 51 per cent.

The arrangement between Helkon and Newmarket was mutually beneficial. For Helkon the deal provided access to Newmarket's other business partnerships and to more films to feed the international distribution channels that Helkon had established in the UK, Spain and Italy. For Newmarket Capital Group the injection of capital was important to the company's plans for further expansion into acquisitions and a move into theatrical distribution, which it did with the establishment of Newmarket Films.

Newmarket Films and *Memento*

Although it was unusual for a distribution company to begin with a one-film slate, Newmarket's decision to distribute *Memento* was forced by the fact that the film had been unable to find another US distributor. *Memento* had been in development with Newmarket since 1998 after Aaron Ryder joined the company from Working Title Films. With responsibility for developing new material, Ryder had been impressed with the scripts for *The Mexican* and Christopher Nolan's *Memento*, both of which were subsequently optioned by Newmarket. The initial budget for *Memento* was set at between $3 million, with $6 million, with Newmarket covering the full amount. Once their longstanding relationship was in place, Summit Entertainment was secured to handle the foreign sales. Finally, to allay concerns from within Newmarket that the script might turn into an 'art film', Jennifer and Suzanne Todd were brought in as producers to give the film 'a commercial sensibility'.[31]

The script for *Memento* was written by Christopher Nolan and adapted from a short story by his brother, Jonathan.[32] Christopher Nolan, who had started making films using his father's Super 8 camera at the age of seven, studied literature at University College London. During his undergraduate years he developed a keen interest in narrative and chronology and began to consider questions of narrative flexibility after reading Graham Swift's novel *Waterland*, the structure of which shifts backwards and forwards in time. With film equipment from the university's film society he began to make short films and made *Tarantella* in 1989 which was shown on *Image Union*, the PBS independent film and video showcase in the US. His short film *Larceny* (1996) was screened at the 1996 Cambridge Film Festival and the following year he made *Doodlebug* (1997), which featured on a DVD compilation of films by British directors titled *Cinema 16*. Nolan's first feature was shot on 16 mm and ran for only 70 minutes. *Following* (1998) was made in London and shot on weekends over the course of a year whilst Nolan worked full-time during the week making corporate videos. *Following* was screened at the Toronto Film Festival in 1998 after being picked up by New Wave Films, a finishing fund for low-budget features, and funded for improvements to the sound mix and a 35 mm print.[33] The film received good reviews and won awards at the Newport, Rotterdam and Slamdance Festivals, but struggled to find theatrical distribution due to its length. Eventually, independent distributor Zeitgeist Films picked up *Following* and handled its US theatrical distribution. Though the film did some business at the US box office, grossing over $43,000, the critical attention it received gave Nolan visibility as a director and he was compared by critics to Alfred Hitchcock, David Mamet and Nicolas Roeg.[34]

Originally the plan had been to shoot *Memento* in Montreal to take advantage of tax breaks which could keep production costs down. These plans were changed and with the new Los Angeles location came increased production costs which necessitated cutting the production schedule from thirty to twenty-five days. Having shot his previous feature on weekends over the course of a year, Nolan's working practices presented some concerns for the producers and the Director of Photography, Wally Pfister, who was hired with only two weeks of pre-production remaining. These concerns centred on whether Nolan would be able to shoot the film according to the official schedule 7 September to 8 October 1999.[35] Nolan preferred not to use shot-lists or storyboards, and during filming his previous experience of operating his own camera for *Following* meant that he was more comfortable next to the camera than watching the performance on a monitor.[36] But the main concerns (which proved to be unfounded) centred on whether Nolan would be able to shoot *Memento* within the scheduled time-frame.

Like *Following*, *Memento* struggled to find US distribution, although in the case of the latter this was due to the complexity of the narrative rather than its length. At a time when foreign pre-sales were becoming difficult to secure, particularly without US theatrical distribution in place, *Memento* was able to buck the trend and Summit achieved $4.5 million of pre-sales to international territories which covered the majority of the film's $5 million budget.[37] Undoubtedly foreign pre-sales were helped substantially by Carrie-Ann Moss's role, given the enormous success of the Wachowski brothers' *The Matrix* (1999) in which she had played the character Trinity.[38] By the end of August *The Matrix* had been released in most major territories giving Moss a marketable star status and Summit was able to secure over 50 per cent of the eventual number of international distributors by the time filming *Memento* began in September of that year.

In March 2000 *Memento* was screened in Los Angeles for US distributors but had interest only from Trimark Pictures, a company that the producers felt was inappropriate for the film.[39] The other distributors at the screening found *Memento* too complicated for audiences and thought it would be difficult to sell. A few weeks later Paramount Classics made an offer for the film but this was rejected as it was considered to be too low.[40] With the film unable to secure a suitable US distributor, Tyrer and Ball decided to expand Newmarket's distribution activities beyond the home entertainment market and into theatrical distribution. Newmarket brought in Bob Berney as a consultant, from independent distributor IFC, to oversee the film's release and *Memento* eventually went into selected theatres in New York and Los Angeles in March 2001. On Berney's advice Newmarket met the full costs of the marketing budget, initially estimated at $5 million but eventually rising to $8 million. *Memento* opened in the US on limited release on 16 March 2001 and after nine weeks, it was on 445 screens and reporting the ninth highest box office returns for the weekend starting 11 May and the third highest weekend screen average with $2,734. This trailed only the averages of *The Mummy Returns* (Sommers, 2001) and *A Knight's Tale* (Helgeland, 2001) which recorded $9,894 and $5,540, respectively. The following week after the release of *Shrek* (Adamson and Jenson, 2001) which went straight to the top spot, grossing over $42 million on its opening weekend, *Memento* slipped just one place to tenth position. It is salient to note that *Memento* was now in its tenth week of release yet still maintained the fifth highest weekend screen average with $2,645, behind the four highest grossing films of that weekend: *Shrek*, *The Mummy Returns*, *A Knight's Tale* and *Angel Eyes* (Mandoki, 2001). Returns for the next weekend improved as *Memento*, on 531 screens, yielded an increased per screen average of $3,719 and, in its twelfth week on release, it was recording the tenth highest box office gross.[41]

Memento was, by all accounts, a success and by July 2001 Newmarket had the leading market share for limited releases at the box office.[42] With a marketplace comprised of 239 films on limited release totaling $160.8 million in box office revenue, Newmarket had a 13.3 per cent share which equated to $21.4 million from a single film. This was all the more remarkable for Newmarket when compared with Lions Gate, which had ten films on limited release but only 12.5 per cent of the total box office. Newmarket was also ahead of Sony Classics with seventeen releases and an 11 per cent share, Fine Line with four releases and a 7.5 per cent share and Miramax with nine films on limited release but claiming only 5 per cent of the market. *Memento* ended 2001 as the indie hit of the year and earned $25.5 million from its domestic theatrical release. However, the aftermarket for *Memento* eclipsed the film's theatrical takings. Released by Columbia TriStar Home Entertainment in September 2001, *Memento* generated over $48 million in video rentals in its first fifty days of release, achieving seventh place in the top 25 rentals chart in October 2001, and by the end of December that year had realised $59.5 million in combined VHS and DVD rental revenue.[43] The exclusive pay TV rights were licensed by Sony Pictures Entertainment to the digital cable channel Starz! for $3.5 million the following March.[44]

After the success of *Memento*, Newmarket teamed up with Bob Berney and IFC for the company's second release in 2001, *Donnie Darko* (Kelly, 2001). The film opened on fifty-eight screens in October 2001 but earned only $110,494 on its opening weekend. The 9/11 attacks which occurred a month prior to its release were blamed for its poor box office performance in the US and *Donnie Darko* closed at the end of 2001 taking just over $400,000. *Donnie Darko* had been released through a service deal with IFC that took advantage of the company's existing distribution structure and there was some speculation in the trade press as to whether or not Newmarket would move fully into distribution. After *Donnie Darko*'s disappointing box office performance Tyrer and Ball announced in early 2002 that Newmarket planned to continue with its film investment business. A few months later, however, it was announced that Newmarket was officially moving into theatrical distribution. In an interview Tyrer stated that the change in direction was because 'intelligent independent films, including our release *Memento*, clearly have a demand in today's marketplace'.[45] In July of that year, Berney announced that he was leaving IFC Films to head up the new distribution division at Newmarket, which planned to release between eight and ten films a year. A couple of months after he joined Newmarket, Beth English, who had worked with Berney and overseen the release of the indie blockbuster *My Big Fat Greek Wedding* (J. Zwick, 2002), also left IFC Films to join the new distribution division as manager of publicity charged with responsibility for overseeing all the release campaigns as well as the company's corporate identity.

In 2003 Newmarket Films released the Sundance Film Festival Audience Award winner *Real Women Have Curves* (Cardoso, 2002), *Spun* (Akerlund, 2002), *Lilya 4-ever* (Moodysson, 2002), *Elsker dig for evigt* [*Open Hearts*] (Jensen 2002) and *Whale Rider* (Caro, 2002). From these *Whale Rider*, on limited release and playing on only 556 screens at its widest release, returned the strongest box office figures with $20.7 million. In 2004 Newmarket handled the distribution of *Monster* (Jenkins, 2003) and *The Passion of the Christ*, which grossed £34 million and $370 million respectively, garnering *Passion*, in 2004, the title of most successful indie film of all time. Whilst the distribution of *Passion* substantially elevated Newmarket's profile in the industry, Berney was identified as the driving force behind Newmarket's success. In 2005 New Line and HBO acquired Newmarket's theatrical distribution unit leaving the film finance arm and Newmarket's film library in Tyrer and Ball's ownership. The New Line/HBO venture created a new specialty unit for major Time Warner, which was later named Picturehouse and headed by Bob Berney.

Conclusion

From its founding in 1994, Newmarket has occupied an interesting position in contemporary American cinema, premised on the company's chameleon-like ability to adapt to the changes in the sector and shift from independent financier to producer, into home entertainment and theatrical distributor, then a return to financier and producer. The company entered the distribution arena at a time when Miramax, which had dominated independent distribution, had changed its focus and was concentrating on larger budget films. This gave Newmarket and other independent distributors the opportunity to exploit the mid-range end of the market. The company's theatrical distribution career began with *Memento*, and between 2001 and 2005 Newmarket was able to claim a number of crossover successes. The acquisition of its distribution unit in 2005 by HBO and New Line was made to secure the services of Berney who had overseen all of Newmarket's distribution successes. In this sense the acquisition was not of a company 'brand', as was the case of Disney's purchase of Miramax, but of a key individual with marketing expertise and an in-depth knowledge of the independent sector. The acquisition was, however, part of the ongoing fluid and mobile culture of company formations and alliances which had become a feature of the sector and, in broader terms, across the cultural industries.

As such, Newmarket's establishment, diversification and expansion cannot be detached from a much wider economic and political context. An international shift in investment away from declining manufacturing industries towards the cultural industries had been facilitated by the dominance of neo-liberalism and accompanying free market policy changes which dominated the 1980s and 1990s. Alongside other forms of cultural production, the film industry represented new investment possibilities which had additional benefits. As David Hesmondhalgh points out:

> The cultural industries were more than just another investment opportunity though. Increasingly they came to be seen as a *prestigious* form of making profits as the entertainment industries came to be perceived as a key economic sector, at least in North America and Europe.[46]

Investment in the cultural industries was thus part of the shift towards mobile global capital enabled by looser international economic policy and, prior to the founding of Newmarket, Tyrer and Ball were already well established within this new landscape, working in LA as entertainment financiers for the Japanese Daiwa bank.

The formation and expansion of Newmarket Capital Group and of the independent sector were enabled by a wider economic context of financial deregulation and the resultant rise of foreign investment into cultural production. In the case of American film this investment came most notably from Japanese and later German investment. Moreover, emphasis on deregulation, which occurred within the telecommunications sector, coupled with free market policy changes, led to a proliferation of channels carrying cultural content. This was apparent, for instance, in the deregulation of European television which represented a ready market for American product and a new avenue for financing opportunities. In terms of economic and cultural deregulation, Newmarket benefited directly via its agreement with Helkon from the rapid growth of the post-unification media landscape in Germany and the resultant international flow of capital and cultural products. Importantly, these changes facilitated Newmarket's move into distribution with Newmarket Films and *Memento*.

How then to conceive of Newmarket and *Memento*'s status as independent when Newmarket's independence is more accurately described as relations of 'interdependence'. To borrow from Hesmondhalgh, 'interdependence' relates to the complex networks of licensing, financing and distribution formed between small and large companies which became characteristic of cultural production in the 1980s.[47] Such alliances have proved beneficial for both 'majors' and 'independents', allowing risk to be shared and competition to be co-opted. As a boutique financier, Newmarket was involved in financing across the film spectrum from studio to art-house projects, thereby operating within a network of small companies and large corporations to form strategic alliances on a project-by-project basis. Its strategy of working with reputable independent producers and forming calculated alliances with Summit, Columbia, Universal and Original Films as well as the relationship between Newmarket and Helkon exemplified webs of interdependence based on the flexible international movement of capital and cultural products.[48] In the case of Newmarket and its range of strategic collaborations, the binary of independent–major, and by extension autonomous–dependent, alternative–mainstream, cannot adequately account for such a multiplicity of formations. This is not to say that independence and 'indie' no longer have meaning. The marketing of 'independent' film and the presence of 'indie' as a product category across multiple cultural forms, including for instance music, demonstrates quite clearly that independence in all its registers continues to have important cultural weight. At the same time there is a nebulous quality whereby independence can be yoked to many different practices, affiliations and products which obfuscate any simple or singular definition. In this case, it may be more useful to conceive of independence as deterritorialised from a specific mode of production and reterritorialised by particular formations and alliances, and *Memento* as a product of reterritorialising affiliations between global mainstreams and local substreams facilitated by the neo-liberal climate within which such constellations could occur.

2 Searching for a Slam Dunk: Marketing *Memento*

They're searching for the indie equivalent of a slam dunk . . . But I think there's always a way to sell a good movie. And this one's not esoteric – it's a murder-mystery!

Christopher Nolan.[1]

That *Memento* struggled to find domestic distribution revealed certain assumptions that distributors held about independent film and its audiences at the beginning of the twenty-first century. US distributors had concerns that American audiences would find the narrative difficult to understand and that *Memento* would be an especially difficult film to market. This had not been the case with European distributors, many of which had bought rights at the script stage. Summit Entertainment, which had a long-standing partnership arrangement with Newmarket, had been successful in securing pre-sales in European territories which covered $4.5 million of the initial $5 million production costs on the strength of the screenplay alone. However, US distributors were convinced that *Memento* would not be appropriate for their audiences, claiming that it was 'too smart' and suggesting instead that the film was more suited to a European market already culturally predisposed to art-house films.[2] The response reflected a general feeling on the part of US distributors that *Memento* leant too far towards the art-house end of the independent spectrum and highlighted the extent to which American distributors had become cautious about niche films, and were looking instead for independent films with a strong potential for crossover success.[3] The balance between 'art house' and 'commercial' was a particularly tricky one, but many wanted to emulate Miramax's strategy for success with 'art-house films for a multiplex audience' – in other words, independent films that would play well in the larger urban theatres.

The distributors' response to *Memento* at the screenings in March

2000 surprised Jennifer and Suzanne Todd, who had been chosen by Newmarket to steer *Memento* away from being too esoteric and give the film commercial credibility. This had translated into a number of key decisions being taken at the pre-production stage and to these ends the producers were pivotal in the final redraft of the screenplay, the design of a twenty-five-day production schedule, the choice of locations, and in assembling both crew and cast for the film. Yet despite their input and commercial credentials, the only offers that the film received were, as we saw in chapter 1, from Trimark and Paramount Classics. The producers immediately rejected both offers on the grounds that they were too low and inappropriate for the film.[4] In an interview in 2001, William Tyrer stated: 'If we had an offer for $8 million we would have said "fine", but that $8 million offer never came. People thought it was too difficult, too obscure, and had no commercial potential.'[5] Thus, whilst the feedback from the distributors, including from Miramax and Artisan, was extremely positive and extolled the virtues of the film, cast and director, the consensus was that *Memento* would not make money.[6]

In an interview for *Film Threat* in March 2001, Steven Soderbergh asserted that *Memento*'s struggle to find a distributor had 'signaled the death of the independent film movement'. He commented, 'I watched it and came out of there thinking "That's it. When a movie this good can't get released, then, it's over".'[7] His judgement reflected a broad concern across the sector that independent film was facing a crisis. In fact a similar sentiment had been expressed six years earlier by producer Ted Hope, who argued that the marketplace for independent film had altered to reflect mainstream tastes, leaving no room for niche films. The problem was threefold: first, distributors were too concerned with finding films with mass market appeal; second, the studios exerted too much control over the independent apparatus; and third, there was 'virtually no American audience for art films, political films or non-narrative films'.[8] According to Hope, the main predicament faced by the independent sector was that distributors routinely imposed the logic and tastes of the mass market on independent film, effectively eroding the idiosyncratic elements of personal vision, unique aesthetic and independent spirit that distinguished it from the commercial Hollywood product.

At the core of the distribution problems facing independent film was the question of marketability which underpinned the majority of acquisition decisions. Distributors were particularly keen to find films with marketable properties, on the assumption that such films had a greater chance of grossing over $2 million at the box office.[9] As a result, many distributors had become involved in financing and producing in order to have control over a film and the chance to shape – to a greater or lesser extent depending on the distributor – its marketable properties at an early stage of pre-production. By 2001, Artisan, Fine Line, Fox Searchlight, Lions Gate, Miramax, Screen Gems and USA Films all relied on a mix of productions and acquisitions to make up their release slates for the year. Even with a degree of control over marketable elements though, productions and co-productions involved a high level of risk, as they were expensive to develop and often put a larger investment at stake than did an acquisition. In addition to having a mix of productions and acquisitions, companies such as Miramax and Lions Gate also opted for a combination of art-house titles on limited release and 'commercial releases', independent films considered to have 'breakout potential' that would play on more than 1,000 screens.[10] According to Soderbergh and Hope, however, the drive for commercial success was detrimental to the sector, leading Hope to propose that 'the logic of the studio film . . . is slowly colonizing our consciousness'.[11] It was this logic that led US distributors to pass on *Memento*.

To put the concerns of Soderbergh and Hope into context it is salient to consider that by 1995 distribution and marketing practices had changed, along with the box office expectations for independent film. By the mid-1990s the major independents Miramax and New Line/ Fine Line were firmly established as key players in independent distribution, whilst Fox Searchlight, the new specialty division of Twentieth-Century-Fox, made the majors' presence in the independent arena all the more visible. For its first release in 1995, Fox Searchlight invested $500,000 in the $26,000 feature *The Brothers McMullen* (Burns, 1995) for post-production costs which included blowing up the original 16 mm negative to 35 mm for theatrical release.[12] *The Brothers McMullen* won the Sundance Grand Jury Prize, took over $1 million on its opening weekend and eventually grossed $10 million at the domestic box office. With the establishment of Fox Searchlight, the majors began a large-scale move into the independent sector, with Paramount, Sony and MGM following Twentieth-Century-Fox's lead and creating their own specialty divisions by the end of the 1990s. This move had a direct impact on distribution in the sector as equity investment from the majors brought about changes to marketing budgets and strategies.

Following Disney's acquisition of Miramax, there were widespread concerns voiced by other distributors that the financial cushion provided by the parent company would enable Miramax to increase its marketing budget and outspend the smaller independents. In general, independent budgets could not compete with the marketing spend on a typical Hollywood production which was, in 1992, around $11.4 million against an average production cost of $29 million. In comparison, the average independent marketing budget was between $300,000 and $5 million for films with highly variable production costs – anything between $7,000 and $10 million.[13] On the basis that, in 1993, a thirty-second advertising spot on ABC during the top-rated television programme of that year, *Home Improvement*, cost $325,000, mass-circulation media such as network television advertising was clearly well beyond the reach of most independents. [14]In 1993, Bob Berney, then senior vice president of marketing and distribution at Triton Pictures and the person who would eventually design the marketing strategy for *Memento*, noted that when it came to marketing budgets, 'indies have to work twice as hard for half the money'.[15] By 1995, the gap between typical Hollywood and independent marketing budgets had widened even further, with an average spend of $17 million for a Hollywood film compared to a static $300,000–900,000 for an independent.[16] As independent films were already struggling to compete with the studios' product for screens and audiences, additional pressure from the 'major independents', Miramax and New Line, as well as the increasing encroachment by the majors into the sector in the form of specialty divisions, further troubled the smaller companies. Unable to find equity investment, distributors such as Triton Pictures, which had released *American Heart* (Bell, 1992) and the documentary features *Heart of Darkness: A Filmmaker's Apocalypse* (Bahr, Hickenlooper and Coppola, 1991) and *A Brief History of Time* (Morris, 1991), could not match the budgets of the major independents or the majors' classics divisions, such as Sony Pictures Classics and Samuel Goldwyn Company. Triton Pictures, which had lost its Japanese backing in early 1993, was one of the smaller specialty distributors squeezed out of the marketplace during the 1990s. The company's founders, Jonathan Dana and Jeff Ivers, commented on Triton's demise in an interview in 1993, stating that 'the realities of today's marketplace require a level of resources greater than we currently have available to us'.[17] Triton, regarded in the trade press as 'a significant challenger to the industry stalwarts in the theatrical distribution business', was unable to survive and the company's closure demonstrated that changing sector economics were having a profound effect on niche theatrical distributors.[18]

Concerns that Miramax would dominate indie distribution by virtue of its affiliation to Disney were realised with the marketing strategy for *Pulp Fiction* in 1994.[19] Part of the strategy for the film included a wide opening release in 1,338 theatres and television advertising that translated into an estimated marketing expenditure of between $5 million and $8 million, a figure that equalled the film's estimated production costs of $8 million.[20] The release for *Pulp Fiction* followed the release patterns used by the majors. Typically, an independent film opened through a platform release, relying heavily on critical reviews and allowing word of mouth to build, a strategy that kept the costs of prints and advertising (p&a) to a minimum. A wide release, playing on more than 600 screens nationally and accompanied by a television advertising campaign, was a more costly venture requiring a significantly higher p&a investment. Prior to the release of *Pulp Fiction*, Miramax had opened other successful films such as *The Crying Game* (Jordan, 1992), *sex, lies, and videotape* (Soderbergh, 1989) and *The Piano* (Campion, 1993) on six, four and four screens respectively, with *The Crying Game* and *The Piano* eventually playing on 1,097 and 671 screens at their widest release and *sex, lies and videotape* staying on limited release on 534 screens. *Pulp Fiction* opened and stayed on wide release, eventually playing on 1,494 screens to finish as the ninth top grossing film of 1994 and the highest grossing independent film, exceeding $100 million at the domestic box office. The top grossing film of that year from the majors, *Forrest Gump* (Zemeckis, 1994, distributed by Paramount), grossed $329 million and opened on 1,595 screens, 257 screens more than *Pulp Fiction*, playing on 2,365 screens at its widest release. The other top grossing films of the year similarly opened on wide release, with *True Lies* (Cameron, 1994, distributed by Twentieth Century Fox) opening on 2,368 screens, *The Santa Clause* (Pasquin, 1994, distributed by Buena Vista Pictures) opening on 2,138 screens and *The Flintstones* (Levant, 1994, distributed by Universal Pictures) opening on 2,498 screens. However, Miramax did not only pursue commercial films on wide release and, in contrast to *Pulp Fiction*, in the same year Miramax chose a platform release strategy for *Clerks* (Smith, 1994), which opened on two screens playing on ninety-six screens at its widest release, and for *Bullets Over Broadway* (Allen 1994), which also opened on two screens and eventually moved to 278 screens. Although the marketing for each film was individually designed according to the budget and target audience, differences in the strategies adopted for *Clerks* and *Bullets Over Broadway* and *Pulp Fiction* emphasised some broad distinctions between the handling of 'art-house' independent films and 'commercial' independent titles.

Platform release for independent titles kept the p&a costs relatively low and also reduced the number of people needed to manage the circulation of prints and box office collections. Taking a film from city to city, a platform release relied on a film staying in a theatre for more than four weeks and was also heavily dependent on critical reviews, both of which were vital to give a film time to build an audience by word of mouth. Los Angeles and New York represented the twin poles of the art-house circuit and critics' reviews in the presses of these cities, which could reach a core older upscale audience, were a significant aspect of the marketing for an independent film. In comparison, a 'commercial' independent that opened on more than 600 screens was more expensive to market with a greatly increased number of prints in circulation nationally which necessitated greater use of mass and specialised media to advertise the film. In the case of a film such as *The Crying Game*, a strategic and later refocused marketing plan allowed the film to cross over from limited release on the art-house circuit and into wide release. However, breakout successes such as *The Crying Game* were not common and, in broad terms, the art-house theatre circuit was crucial to platform release strategies, allowing time for word of mouth to build and offering an alternative type of film and venue to the Hollywood product and mass-oriented multiplex and megaplex theatres.[21]

The relationship between the art-house circuit and its audience was more intimate than that between the multiplex and its audience, with art-house theatres developing an audience through mailing lists, newsletters and special events such as lecture tours. In contrast, the mulitiplexes tended to rely on Hollywood advertising in the popular media to address an audience and, despite creating art-house screens within megaplexes, theatres on the commercial circuit did little to promote films or build audiences for specialty films. Instead, multiplexes worked to a model that required films to find an audience during the opening week and it made little business sense for these theatres to wait for an audience to grow when a screen could be used to show a wide-release studio film with the promise of much higher immediate returns. For instance, *Breaking The Waves* (von Trier, 1996), which was distributed by October Films, opened on six screens, one of which was the Sony Lincoln Square multiplex, which pulled the film after the opening week following disappointing box office returns from its first weekend.

There was a clear push towards marketable elements in independent films during the 1990s and the rise of specialised media offered distributors new opportunities to reach target audiences without having to resort to expensive mass-circulation media. The fragmentation of US radio in the early 1990s was particularly significant for niche advertising to target markets and the revenues generated from radio advertising reflected this, recording over $9.4 billion in 1993.[22] Radio advertising was cost effective as stations used demographic research to slice the market into clearly defined segments, thereby giving better access to a target market than that offered by the more expensive mass-circulation media. Similarly, growth in cable television and targeted magazines offered cheaper alternatives to broadcast television and newspapers for independents keen to reach specific markets. Miramax and New Line proved to be particularly adept at marketing through targeted advertising and promotions. For the US release of *Como agua para chocolate* (*Like Water For Chocolate*, Arau, 1992), a Spanish language film with no stars, the film was marketed by Miramax to Hispanic and art-house audiences through advertising and promotions on the Spanish-language network Telemundo and advertising on Cable News Network respectively. In keeping with the traditional release strategy for art-house films and to exploit the film's critical reviews, *Like Water for Chocolate* opened in New York and Los Angeles theatres. In another example of a targeted approach, New Line promoted *Menace II Society* (Hughes, 1993) to a black teen core audience on Black Entertainment Television and MTV with a marketing budget of $2 million for the $3 million film.[23] Even with cheaper targeted specialised media available to independents, however, advertising remained expensive, with a radio ad during a top-rated show costing around $3,200 in 1993.[24] Marketing independent films required ingenuity to reap the largest rewards from a small budget and this often meant that strategies relied on grassroots promotions, director-led publicity and carefully timed release dates, as well as the usual apparatus of festivals, print, radio and television advertising, (one-sheet) posters and critical reviews.

Marketing independence

Whilst niche marketing was a significant strategy for independent film, independent filmmakers became central to film marketing as did the cultural weight of the term 'independent'. This in turn generated much debate within the industry and from critics and academics, concerned with defining what independence meant. The marketing of independent film produced a public discourse of independence which fed into debates increasingly engaged with shifts within the sector, the over-commercialisation and institutionalisation of independence, issues of authenticity and possibilities for providing a real alternative to Hollywood. Dependence on the majors complicated definitions of 'independent' film where the term had been taken to mean independence in all aspects of finance, production and distribution from the major conglomerates and, by the mid-1990s, a time of unparalleled success for the independent sector, the terms 'independent' and 'independent film' were hotly debated. Yet whilst definitions of independence were in flux, at the same time an institutional apparatus was mobilised around the construction of a more stable and coherent public understanding of independent film. This arose because the terms 'indie' and 'independent' were considered to function as marketing labels and part of a strategy of product differentiation in the film marketplace. Independent film had to have some coherence as a commercial marketing category to distinguish the product from mainstream studio films in order to target, as Justin Wyatt notes, a new segment of 'upscale, educated' consumers 'aged twenty-five to forty-five'.[25] On one hand, this meant in the case of the major independents that relationships with a major parent company were necessarily played down to ensure that independent films could be positioned as a distinct product. Thus Miramax's public distance from Disney can be understood as part of a broader strategy to ensure that the Miramax 'brand' retained its valuable and marketable identity as an independent company. And in terms of maintaining product differentiation Dimension Films, established by the Weinstein brothers to distribute commercial genre films, preserved a distinction from the specialty product associated with Miramax and the family-oriented entertainment of Disney.[26] Similarly, in relation to product differentiation Newmarket established a clear distance between its home entertainment distribution arm with its focus on genre films and its theatrical distribution interests focused on niche audiences for independent film. Will Tyrer commented that *Memento* was an 'intelligent film', and in doing so Newmarket aligned itself with a discourse of independent film that had resonance with an educated, discerning consumer.[27]

The maintenance of product differentiation within the marketplace relied on the maturation of an institutional apparatus that, Justin Wyatt argues, enabled independent cinema to become established as 'a commercial marketing category in itself . . . [able to] support itself through its own marketing apparatus, by arguing, however tenuously, that 'independent' is superior to studio output'.[28] This independent marketing apparatus included film festivals, awards, art-house theatre circuits, critical reviews, specialist print publications and television channels, and by 1999 the Internet, and therefore reflexively validated itself and the status of particular films and filmmakers as 'independent'. The prominence of the Sundance Film Festival within the institutional apparatus for instance, authorised its self-definition as 'a non-profit organization dedicated to the discovery and development of independent artists and audiences' and reflexively legitimated the independent status of films screened there.[29] And, despite appropriation by the majors via the major independents, the apparatus was by the mid-1990s mature enough to successfully produce authorised definitions of independence that were self-serving.

One of the industrial categories supported by the independent institutional apparatus is film authorship and the construction of the independent director as an *auteur*, which Yannis Tzioumakis notes is an 'extratextual authorial agency' that can enhance the 'independent spirit and status' of a film.[30] Whilst festival success and awards were vital to *Following* and *Memento* in marketing terms, the autonomy of the filmmaker working outside or on the margins of the mainstream was also marketable and contributed to what Geoff King has referred to as 'the romance of independent cinema'.[31] Accounts of *Following*, referred to in reviews as an 'ultra-low budget', fitted the first-time indie filmmaker narrative so well that one journalist noted that the film was 'the sort of no-budget indie début whose merits are in danger of being eclipsed by its underdog-made-good backstory'.[32]

Narratives of independent filmmakers creating low- or no-budget films, then being 'discovered' at a film festival and finding commercial success, were a discernible feature of the mediated discourse of independence during the 1990s. Such stories contributed to a myth of independent film in which talent and artistic endeavour, working outside the mainstream system and driven by a love for film, were eventually recognised and rewarded. This notion of the struggling independent director who found commercial success had a newfound visibility, deployed and propagated throughout various trade publications with the potential to cross over into mass-circulation media.[33] Consider, for instance, a 1993 *Filmmaker* interview with Robert Rodriguez:

If Robert Rodriguez didn't exist, independent filmmakers would have to invent him – an unknown 23-year-old makes a terrific first feature for $7,000, is snapped up by ICM, signed to a two-picture deal by Columbia, and then applauded at the Telluride and Toronto film festivals.[34]

Picked up by *Time Magazine* the against-all-odds story of Rodriguez and *El Mariachi* continued to circulate:

Now all Hollywood is calling Rodriguez because Columbia Pictures is distributing his movie. Not bad for a 24-year-old who raised nearly half the film's budget (okay, $3,000) by serving as a 'lab rat' in a medical-research project in his hometown of Austin, Texas.[35]

And *MovieMaker* recounted a similar success story about Scott Mosier and Kevin Smith in a 1993 article, stating in the opening paragraph:

Now signed to feature deals with Universal and Miramax, Smith and Mosier's début offers the hope that even in the studio-controlled multiplex jungle, any nobody who makes a good movie – even without money, experience or connections – can have their big time moviemaking dreams fall right into their lap.[36]

Such narratives translated well into mass-media forms and, in addition to Rodriguez and Mosier and Smith, the breakthrough successes of others such as Steven Soderbergh, Spike Lee and Daniel Myrick, and Eduardo Sánchez, and particularly Quentin Tarantino, offered similar opportunities for rags-to-riches stories of filmmakers' working outside the Hollywood system and remaining true to their personal vision. In this sense, the 'indie filmmaker success story' reduced a diverse range of practices, activities, aesthetics and ideologies into a narrative of independence that had resonance in the popular media, thereby offering the potential to affiliate the mainstream media to the independent marketing apparatus.

Whilst such stories offered coherence to a varied set of independent practices, disapproval of the continual reworking of the struggling independent filmmaker narrative highlighted tensions between the various institutional definitions of independence.[37] Criticisms were levelled at institutions such as the Independent Feature Project (IFP), founded in 1979 as a non-profit organisation for independent filmmakers, for promoting the myth of 'the rags-to-riches tale of the first-time filmmaker' and ignoring political distinctions between filmmakers and filmmaking practices in their quarterly publication *Filmmaker*.[38] The magazine, established in 1992, claimed to be 'by filmmakers, on filmmakers, for filmmakers'.[39] However, critics of *Filmmaker* argued that independent filmmaking should remain true to an ideal of active and self-conscious opposition to dominant media practices at every level – technologically, institutionally, aesthetically, economically and politically – a position that drew heavily on a discourse of independence associated with the New American Cinema.[40] Whilst *Filmmaker* avoided politics in favour of what it referred to as a 'postmodern' view of independent film that 'can herald filmmakers as diverse as Quentin Tarantino to Nina Menkes', a publication such as *Cineaste*, which claimed its position as 'America's leading magazine on the art and politics of the cinema', represented the opposite discourse.

In a 1999 editorial *Cineaste* attacked the marketing practices of Miramax, October Films and Artisan, arguing that film hype had reached such levels that its rhetorical power severely delimited an audience's opportunity to judge a film with any level of critical detachment. In particular, the magazine cited *The Blair Witch Project* (Myrick and Sánchez, 1999) as an example of 'buzz [that] was engendered by another set of movie clichés – the tendency to mythologize plucky, independent filmmakers and their ability to make a movie in eight days with almost no money'.[41] Cynical about the notion of the struggling independent director with a commitment to filmmaking, the magazine stated that 'most American "independent" films are conceived by their directors as stepping stones to an industry career, as audition pieces for the next available studio job for hire'.[42] Another article argued that 'Sundance-independent-*Filmmaker* films have a certain look, story, and budget, critic claims, and the magazine is just one more cog in an inbred marketing machine that ends up at your local multiplex'.[43] Such criticisms, which traced the problematic concept of independence back to Soderbergh's success with *sex, lies, and videotape* at the 1989 Sundance Film Festival, argued that this was the moment when independent film lost its radical political position as an oppositional force to dominant media practices and became a marketing tool.[44]

What debates around film marketing highlighted, critically or otherwise, was that the independent apparatus was increasingly reliant on various forms of interdependence. Moreover, the relations between 'independent' and 'mainstream' were not only part of the marketing of commercial indie films, but also of importance to the various discourses that negotiated 'difference' and legitimised the range of meanings about independent film in circulation. As such, the reterritorialisation of independence took place within the discursive practices of differentiation where 'independence' and 'indie' were deployed to serve various and competing interests. Indie product differentiation did not, however, operate within an independent/mainstream oppositional binary, and whilst the negotiation of such difference played a role, the practices that targeted niche markets attested to a more nuanced appreciation of product differentiation. Within the differentiated independent product were many more layers of difference that recognised an array of group identities targeted through such niche marketing practices. Thus, whilst the older, upscale educated consumer had resonance for the marketing of certain independent products, the strategies employed for *Menace II Society*, *Like Water for Chocolate* and *Memento* recognised other social identities.

Marketing *Memento*

In 1999, film marketing focused on the possibilities offered by the Internet following the phenomenal success of *The Blair Witch Project* (Myrick and Sánchez, 1999), which had used a website as a key element of the film's campaign. The marketing campaign for *The Blair Witch Project*, distributed by Artisan, was designed by John Hegeman with an initial cost of $1.5 million.[45] The campaign used what were widely referred to in the trade press as 'guerrilla marketing tactics'. These included setting up the website www.blairwitch.com and regularly posting footage on it that had been shot for, but not used in, the film. Aimed at a young target audience, promotional teams went to clubs and coffee-houses to raise awareness and build word of mouth by asking people what they knew about 'Blair Witch'. Authentic 'missing' posters were created using photographs of the film's three main characters and the promotion teams also worked on creating awareness of the 'stick-figure', which became a key visual motif. Three thirty-second teaser trailers were revealed over an eighteen-week period, with the third trailer timed to coincide with the release of *Star Wars: Episode I The Phantom Menace* (Lucas, 1999) to reach a maximum audience. Other elements included a documentary-style special on the Sci-Fi Channel *Curse of the Blair Witch* (Myrick and Sánchez, 1999) and the release of a soundtrack CD, despite there being no music in the film. The website was a particularly innovative aspect of the film's marketing and all other promotional materials pointed towards the site, which received three million visitors per day.[46] What was novel about the *Blair*

Witch site was that it continued the film's central premise, blurring the line between fact and fiction and giving visitors a back-story to the film, including details about the missing filmmakers, the myth of the 'Blair Witch', photographs and examples of police evidence.

By late 1999, the Internet was being widely touted as the salvation of independent film, able to level the playing field and allow independent filmmakers to reach a national if not global audience much as a Hollywood film did. Trade publications reported that the Internet would open up new possibilities for film marketing and the idea given credence by people such as Jacques Thelemaque, the president of the Filmmaker's Alliance in Los Angeles, who claimed, 'Where digital production has democratized filmmaking opportunities, the internet has democratized distribution and exhibition opportunities.'[47] Christopher and Jonathan Nolan, aware of the success of *Blair Witch*, decided to use a website as a key aspect of *Memento*'s publicity. Prior to Berney being brought in to handle the marketing and distribution of the film, Jonathan developed the site www.otnemem.com (i.e. memento spelt backwards), working with a New York-based website company.[48]

Originally designed without cast and crew details the website constructed a fragmented back-story for the film's protagonist Leonard. After some introductory screens, the main page of the *Memento* website is in the form of a report torn from a newspaper with a series of words highlighted as links to the rest of the site. The report describes a police murder investigation launched after the discovery of a photograph of a dead body in a room at the Discount Inn. It claims that the police are looking for Leonard Shelby and that someone of the same name escaped from a Bay-area psychiatric facility in September 1998. The highlighted words act as links to various photographs, handwritten notes and reports, fragments of evidence which provide a series of clues that can be pieced together to suggest what happened to Leonard in the period leading up to and following the events depicted in the film. Information on the website includes psychiatric and clinical reports, which state that Leonard and his wife were attacked in February 1997 and that Leonard's initial diagnosis was made in January 1998. Other report fragments confirm that his wife, Catherine, was dead by the time Leonard was admitted to the psychiatric ward whilst, the police and newspapers verify that Catherine survived the attack, was unresponsive at the scene and in a critical condition the following day. From the series of handwritten notes that, it is suggested, are written by Leonard to himself, one scrap of paper dated

11 April 1997 begins: 'She's gone Leonard. Gone for good.'[49] Clicking the word 'Questions' on the main page of the website reveals two scraps of paper, one with the question 'WHO DID I KILL?' and the other a blank piece that the visitor is able to type into. Typing characters' names to the paper returns the visitor to the main page, with the exception of the name 'Teddy'. When entered in the appropriate field, this takes the visitor to a montage of shots and audio from the film followed by the Polaroid images of Teddy, Dodd and Natalie used in the film, and finally a photograph of Leonard.

The extratextual material was, according to Christopher Nolan, a way of taking the experience of *Memento* beyond the film: 'It creates a larger experience than film-makers have to do . . . you can increase people's understanding of the film allowing them to re-experience it again.'[50] The material gave rise to animated discussions in chatrooms and on message boards about what had 'actually' happened. Far from disambiguating *Memento*, the website material intensified the number of hypotheses in circulation about the film, a point that did not escape the attention of Nolan, who remarked, 'When I read the message boards, I saw that people took different bits of information from the site and interpreted them differently . . . It was gratifying to see that happen.'[51]

Berney began to orchestrate the marketing and distribution of *Memento* for Newmarket in July 2000 and incorporated the website into the overall strategy. Before being released in the US, the film opened in the UK, France and Switzerland in October 2000, distributed by Pathé and UGC. Summit Entertainment's involvement ensured that the film's opening was built around certain European film festivals and to coincide with the film's release in the UK it was screened at the Raindance Film Festival, where Christopher Nolan presented a retrospective of his work. Three days after Raindance had opened, in an interview for the BBC, Nolan was asked about the innovative narrative structure. He replied:

Filmmakers should be able to experiment with narrative without alienating the audience and without creating something that's impenetrable. I actually see myself as a very mainstream film maker and always have. Even though you aren't going to get the answers to all of the questions in the film and it is a kind of unsettling film in lots of ways, if you watch it a couple of times it's pretty much all in there.[52]

The film's ambiguity became central to *Memento*'s publicity with the director withholding the definitive account of what happened and suggesting that, if viewed enough times, the answers would become clear. In much the same way, the website continued with the ambivalent theme and whilst it offered a back-story for Leonard, the film's overarching ambiguity was such that definitive accounts based on information gleaned from the website continued to be contested in online debates.

Memento opened on the London art-house circuit on 20 October, playing at the Curzon (Soho), Ritzy (Brixton) and Everyman (Hampstead) in addition to two UGC cinemas, the Odeon (Camden Town), and beyond London in Cambridge, Milton Keynes and Norwich. Using niche media to target audiences, full-page print advertisements were taken out in *Time Out: London*, which used the recursive Leonard and Natalie Polaroid artwork with the tagline 'Some memories are best forgotten'. Christopher Nolan's name was not prominent, being included in the line of credits at the bottom of the ad, with the emphasis, instead, on the names of the principal actors, Guy Pearce, Carrie-Anne Moss and Joe Pantoliano. Two quotes from critics featured at the top and bottom of the main image – from *Uncut Magazine*: 'One of the most compelling and challenging films of this year, you'll be gripped, enthralled and exhausted. A MODERN CLASSIC. UNFORGETTABLE!', and from *FHM*: 'Dazzling, a masterpiece on a par with *The Usual Suspects*'.[53] The reference to *The Usual Suspects* reflected Newmarket's broad expectations for the film's audience. Will Tyrer later commented, 'We thought this film could reach the same audience that supported *The Usual Suspects* and *The Spanish Prisoner*.[54] (Newmarket had provided production financing for *The Usual Suspects*, a commercial 'puzzle film', whilst the audience for *The Spanish Prisoner* was mainly fans of the director David Mamet and 'arthouse/"indie" audiences'.[55]) This target audience encompassed an ambitious range of different social identities, from college kids to older, upscale audiences. To these ends, Newmarket and Berney wanted to cultivate a position between commercial mainstream and art house for the film in the US in the hope of a crossover success. To bridge the art house/commercial divide in the UK, ads from October 2000 utilised signifiers such as 'masterpiece' and 'modern classic' to speak to an art-house audience whilst Christopher Nolan's insistence during publicity interviews that he should be thought of as a mainstream director was an important counter to the idea that *Memento* was too arty, impenetrable or esoteric.

Memento opened in North America in March 2001 after its début at the Sundance Film Festival in January. The timing was designed to maximise the word of mouth and buzz that had been generated by the European release and Internet campaign. In addition, *Memento* exploited a gap in the market for a film aimed at younger college audiences, opening against *Exit Wounds* (Bartkowiak, 2001), *Enemy at the Gates* (Annaud, 2001), *American Desi* (Pandya, 2001) and *Gabriela* (Miller, 2001), with Berney noting: 'I think we benefited from an abundance of formulaic fare. That's one reason we stayed around. We certainly were completely different.'[56] Berney planned a platform release, opening the film on ten screens in New York and Los Angeles, a combination of art-house and suburban commercial theatres, again in the hope that the film would cross over easily. The release pattern took the film to fifteen screens in the second week, with slow expansion to 250 screens by the sixth week and to 531 screens at its widest release in the eleventh week. To attract a younger audience, colleges were targeted, beginning with New York University, and Berney chose an aggressive publicity campaign which included radio and television as well as personal appearances by Joe Pantoliano on college campuses to capitalise on public awareness of him as Ralph Cifaretto in the HBO television series *The Sopranos*.

Print advertisements in *LA Weekly* a week prior to the film's release used the recursive artwork that had featured in the early UK marketing campaign in an advertisement that ran over three pages and approximated a developing Polaroid that gained more detail and information from page to page. On the first page, the pale, 'undeveloped' image had only 'otnemem.com' written beneath it. On page 2 the recursive photograph was partially 'developed' as the ad built up with the addition above the image of a quote from *Entertainment Weekly*: 'Breathless Film Noir!' A second quote was included on the third page: a 'Two Thumbs Up!' review rating from the Disney-ABC Domestic Television film review television programme *Ebert & Roeper and the Movies*. By the final page the Polaroid image was fully 'developed' with the film title, names of the three principal actors, tagline, main credits and the film's recent festival selection history at Toronto, Venice and Sundance. Beneath the website address, the text 'Exclusive Engagements Open Friday, March 16'. Other than the website address, genre was emphasised in the early US ad with reference to the film's status as *noir* appearing first. *Roger* Ebert's, 'two thumbs up' judgement, trademarked as a phrase in 1989 to retain its credibility and prestige, was included as a signifier of quality which acquired widespread cultural resonance from its inclusion in the influential syndicated television programme. *Memento*'s selection for screening at the Toronto, Venice and Sundance festivals also operated as signifiers of quality within a discourse of independence wherein festival presence and competition wins remained valuable for independent film marketing, connoting prestige.

In the *Village Voice* a half-page advertisement for *Memento*'s release in New York again used the recursive image. In this ad, however, there was even greater emphasis on the plot, using critics' quotes ('Dazzling reverse-gear thriller' and 'Mesmerizing mind-bender') as well as the qualitative recommendations, '*Memento*' is easily the best film so far this year' and 'One of the must-see films of the year'. The US print advertisements favoured the enigmatic aspects of *Memento*, in the use of the recursive imagery and quotes that referenced the film's innovative structure, whilst the early UK ads focused on markers of distinction such as the film being a 'classic', a 'masterpiece'. The US ads also incorporated signifiers of esteem including the two thumbs reference and the film's screenings at prestigious festivals. Publicity interviews with Christopher and Jonathan Nolan and the cast also tended to focus on the complexity of the narrative and the film's ambiguity, and often highlighted the disagreements between those involved with the film about what actually happened. In an interview with the Nolan brothers for the radio programme *All Things Considered*, when asked about the ending Christopher suggested that his view of the 'objective truth' is there if the film is watched enough times. Jonathan's response was directed to Christopher and referred to an interview at the Venice Film Festival:

That's why I got so upset at you for betraying the logic of the film by, at one point, early on, tipping your hand and revealing your interpretation of events, which just for the record, I might point out I wholeheartedly disagree with.[57]

Disputes such as these between the director and the author of the original story, *Memento Mori*, heightened intrigue around the film and further fanned the flames of debate that were in circulation on the Internet about whether the film did indeed have an objective truth. Opening the film on the art-house circuit in both the UK and the US, using a platform release pattern, targeting college audiences and an upscale educated audience that Newmarket associated with films such as *The Spanish Prisoner* as well as the more mainstream commercial possibilities that the film suggested (being likened to *The Usual Suspects*) *Memento* was marketed as an intelligent independent film with 'alternative' appeal. In an article about Bob Berney, the *Washington Post* said, 'Berney's hits have all started as often provocative niche pictures and ended as movies people felt they had to see in order to be culturally literate.'[58] In other words, Berney designed marketing strategies that enabled independent films to cross over and find a mainstream audience.

Conclusion

Berney's final marketing spend for the film was $8.5 million.[59] Alongside trailers which were placed on cable television channels as well as on the Yahoo and MSN websites, the film's website was a key aspect of its marketing supported by grassroots strategies such as handing out postcards with only the web address, otnemem.com, at festivals and bulk mailing of Polaroid photographs to randomly chosen homes, again carrying only the website details. Each of these strategies proved cost-effective and vital to building word of mouth. As critical support for the film grew and the film's ending continued to be widely debated online, publicity interviews with those involved in the film exploited the ambiguity by publicly refusing to agree on what really happened. With interest growing in Nolan as the writer-director, publicity began to focus on his filmmaking history, and the narrative of the filmmaker working against the odds to complete his first feature, *Following*, which became integral to the wider discourse on *Memento*. That Nolan's first two features experimented with narrative as well as both being indebted to *film noir* did not go unnoticed and the comparisons between Nolan and other *auteur* filmmakers, such as Alfred Hitchcock and Nicolas Roeg, were part of an emergent critical discourse. *Memento*'s platform release following key festival screenings and the later niche advertising on radio, cable television and in specialist publications, broadly followed the independent release patterns for indie films on the art-house circuit. However, the film's crossover success was also due to the targeting of a young college audience and its strategic placement in cinemas close to large campuses. To coincide with this, Pantoliano also made numerous personal appearances at various colleges. Different taste markers were utilised in later advertisements such as the one that appeared in the *Los Angeles Times* in June 2001 and used the Internet Movie Database Top 250 movies list as a background, with *Memento* emboldened and underlined at number twelve in the list. An image of Natalie holding open Leonard's shirt to reveal the words 'raped and murdered' across his chest were positioned in the bottom right corner with a listing of the soundtrack, which featured music from Paul

Oakenfold, Radiohead, Moby and Bjork. Adopting a strategy similar to that used for *Blair Witch*, none of the tracks by these artists appeared in the film but were included on the soundtrack CD entitled *Memento: Music for and Inspired by the film*.

Such strategies find parallels with recent academic and industry interest in the marketability of 'cool', which Nancarrow, Nancarrow and Page define as 'a form of cultural capital that increasingly consists of insider knowledge about commodities and consumption practices as yet unavailable to the mainstream'.[60] The marketable concept of 'cool' in this sense relies on a cultural product's perceived authenticity, its non-mainstream status, its acceptance by authorised 'leading-edge consumers' and a broad acknowledgement that 'a cool lifestyle can be achieved, to a large extent, through selective consumption'.[61] Aspects of the marketing of *Memento* thus utilised the Internet Movie Database ranking as evidence of the film's rating by 'leading-edge consumers', whilst references to indie and indie/alternative artists and *noir* drew on discourses of commodified cool in popular music and film that were already in circulation.

Memento's marketing strategy also focused on the complex plot, although advertising in the UK and the US used varied taste signifiers that revealed differences in the target audiences. In the UK, middle-brow signifiers of quality, terms such as 'classic' and 'masterpiece', referenced literary discourses and were used in the advertising that accompanied *Memento*'s opening on the London art-house circuit. The US opening favoured a slightly different approach, emphasising the intellectual challenge of the film with references to the complex narrative for the New York release and popularised markers of quality, in the form of the 'two thumbs up' rating for the Los Angeles opening. Other markers of distinction, such as the references to festival screenings, functioned within a discourse of independence wherein the independent apparatus legitimated particular festival appearances as signifiers of quality. As such, a marketable discourse of independence was already in circulation and established independent film more broadly as offering an alternative to the mainstream product. *Memento* exploited this notion of difference and accompanied it with other sets of embedded taste signifiers that spoke through niche advertising to individual social agents.

3 Puzzle Films, Ambiguity and Technologically-enabled Narrative

One day I drank too much coffee and said to myself, 'Well, if you tell the story backwards, then the audience is put in the same position as Leonard. He doesn't know what just happened, but neither do we.'

Christopher Nolan[1]

In the first two months of its limited release, repeat theatrical viewings accounted for 20 per cent of *Memento*'s $7 million box office between March and May 2001.[2] The complex narrative was a crucial aspect of the film's success which drew cinemagoers back to theatres for multiple viewings and, in doing so, contributed substantially to making *Memento* the top grossing independent film and limited release of the year. *Memento* continued to enjoy a lucrative post-theatrical life on DVD as viewers remained intrigued by the film's innovative narrative as well as having the promise of extra features which included a chronological version of the film, hidden as an 'Easter egg', as a further enticement to purchase. Christopher Nolan always intended *Memento* to be a film that would encourage repeat viewings, remarking in one interview: 'if you can make a film that actually does something different the second time you see it; to me that's a fascinating thing.'[3] Any suggestion that the film would repay multiple viewings with definitive answers though was implicitly denied by the actors and director. In press interviews Carrie-Ann Moss and Joe Pantoliano maintained that after many viewings they still had questions about what happened, and the film's production notes persisted with the ambiguity, stating that 'viewers have found that *Memento* stands up to multiple viewings, the mystery deepening, shifting and clarifying each time'.[4] Nolan refused to shed light on the film's ending to the extent that the Special Edition DVD included multiple director's commentaries, each of which suggested different readings of the film. He insisted that, despite seeing the film 'thousands of times', much the same as any audience he would not know where he was in the narrative if he walked into a theatre halfway through a screening. Referring to the film's editing pattern as 'experimental', from the outset Nolan's aim was to make *Memento* deliberately ambiguous and challenging in terms of its narrative organisation.[5]

That *Memento* intentionally goes against the norms of narrative construction is significant. The conditions of cinematic viewing are such that filmmakers have tended to avoid complex temporal reorganisation. A narrative that presents events out of chronological order risks confusing the spectator who, in a theatre, is unable to stop and re-wind the film and therefore has 'only one shot at comprehending the film passing before their eyes'.[6] David Bordwell argues that 'the relentless forward march of stimuli in a film puts an extra strain on the spectator's memory and inferential processes', therefore mixing up the chronological order of events may force the spectator 'to choose between reconstructing story order and losing track of current action'.[7] Yet, despite such risks to narrative comprehension, films that reorder time, rearrange the sequence of events or display narrative complexity have proved appealing to audiences and enjoyed considerable popularity. Apart from *Memento*, *Pulp Fiction*, *21 Grams* (Iñárritu, 2003) *Reservoir Dogs* (Tarantino, 1992), *Run Lola Run* (*Lola Rennt* Tykwer, 1998), *The Butterfly Effect* (Bress and Gruber, 2004) and *Donnie Darko*, for instance have eschewed narrative norms. Moreover, there has been a notable increase in the number of films which employ narrative complexity in one form or another, and significantly many of these have come from the independent sector. Writing about 'puzzle films' as a particular form of complex narrative, Warren Buckland (2009) argues that they are 'a mode of filmmaking that cuts across traditional filmmaking practices' to include those of 'American "independent" cinema, the European and international art film, and certain modes of avant-garde filmmaking'.[8]

Temporal reordering places *Memento* within this larger group of 'puzzle films' which demonstrate a tendency to narrative complexity which has become more common since the 1990s.[9] Although this trend may be fairly recent, antecedents to the latest proliferation of complex storytelling are dispersed throughout the history of cinema. For instance, in his taxonomy of 'alternative plots' in recent films Charles Ramírez Berg (2006) finds forebears in every decade of American film and suggests that there are twelve plot types which can be classified by alternative narrative activity.[10] According to Berg, the forerunners of the 'Backwards Plot', and therefore *Memento*'s precursors, are early trick films such as *Bathing Made Easy* (Hepworth, 1902) and *Building Made Easy; or, How Mechanics Work in the Twentieth Century* (Edison, 1902), whilst a resurgence of interest in reverse plotting in the twenty-first century has given rise to a clutch of films including *Bakha satang* (*Peppermint Candy*, Chang-dong, 2000), *5 × 2* (Ozon, 2004), *Irrévesible* (Noé, 2002) and *Rules of Attraction* (Avary, 2002).[11] Also concerned with locating earlier ventures into narrative complexity, David Bordwell (2006) points to two distinct periods in Hollywood history prior to the 1990s when experiments in storytelling were common; he proposes that narrative innovation is not unique to contemporary cinema but has arisen in the past as a consequence of various economic and artistic factors.[12] 1940–55 and the mid-1960s–1970s were eras of experimentation characterised by unreliable flashbacks, flashbacks within flashbacks, multiple narrators, dream sequences, multiple narrators and ambivalent timeframes, devices instigated by the need for originality and influenced by new generations of directors.[13] Examples of films that used innovative narrative devices during these periods included *Citizen Kane* (Wells, 1941), *How Green Was My Valley* (Ford, 1941), *Stage Fright* (Hitchcock, 1950), *The Locket* (Brahm, 1946), *Laura* (Preminger, 1944), *All About Eve* (Mankiewicz, 1950), *They Shoot Horses, Don't They?* (Pollack, 1969) and *Images* (Altman, 1972).[14] With the later period, exhausted by the mid-1970s, there was a noticeable return to complex storytelling in the final decade of the twentieth century.[15] *Reservoir Dogs* and *Pulp Fiction* pre-empted a renewed willingness by filmmakers to engage with alternative narratives, leading one scholar to attribute the later surge in complex storytelling to the 'Tarantino effect'.[16] Aside from the degree of influence that Tarantino may have had on other filmmakers, the revival of narrative innovation in the 1990s has also been linked to changes and developments in technology, the influence of the Internet and video game non-linearity, and the growth and maturation of the independent sector.

Technological changes in the last decades of the twentieth century led to the expansion of post-theatrical exhibition platforms which continued to develop in the 2000s and provide a profitable after-market for films. Home video technology gave viewers options to pause and review a film, watch the whole film or just particular scenes multiple times to discover details that were not obvious at a first viewing in a cinema. DVD took these possibilities further, with options for multiple or alternative endings as well as bonus features that could enhance the pleasures offered by a film's narrative complexity. Filmmakers exploited the possibilities of home entertainment platforms by including details, such as the five 'subliminal Brad' inserts in *Fight Club* (Fincher, 1999), specifically for the post-theatrical market on DVD.[17] In addition, the inclusion of a director's commentary offered the promise of an authoritative discourse on a complex narrative and implicitly underscored the expectation that the film would be viewed at least twice; without and with the commentary. In his account of the 'mind-game film' Thomas Elsaesser (2009) examines the relationship between home entertainment technology and narrative complexity in some depth and refers to the 'DVD-enabled movie' as a film that 'requires or repays multiple viewings'. Such films, he suggests, have responded to particular industrial conditions, forms of reception and consumer activity where the 'theatrical release or presence on the international film festival circuit prepares for its culturally more durable and economically more profitable afterlife in another aggregate form'.[18] In these terms, complex narratives have a certain economic logic as multiple viewings, either theatrical or post-theatrical, equate to increased revenue.

The phenomenal growth in Internet use and video games may also explain why viewers are better equipped, and even culturally primed, to accommodate non-linearity and narrative complexity. Websites and video games have, over the last two decades, presented new types of cultural experience that challenge the linear conventions of more traditional narrative encounters. The extent to which such technologies have influenced individual filmmakers to experiment with storytelling is less certain, however. Tarantino has argued that the narrative structure of *Reservoir Dogs* was influenced by a more traditional storytelling form, the novel, which can 'go back and forth all the time'.[19] Nonetheless, in addition to film, there has been a noticeable growth in complex narratives in television, with programmes such as *Lost* (2004, ABC) and *Heroes* (2006, NBC), as well as alternative and non-linear narratives in music videos, and multiplayer and interactive narrativity in online gaming, which suggest a wider cultural trend towards unconventional narration.[20] Within this trend there has been a noticeable concentration of narrative complexity in independent films. One reason for the shift towards complex storytelling and alternative narratives in the independent sector since the 1990s has been the need for product differentiation, to distinguish the independent product from Hollywood and its adherence to classical norms of storytelling.[21] This clustering of narrative complexity highlights a relationship between independent film and complex narratives while raising the intriguing issue of how spectators make sense of such films. In both regards, *Memento* offers a particularly fruitful avenue for such exploration. The following section addresses these questions through a detailed analysis of the film framed by David Bordwell's cognitive theory of narrative comprehension.

Narrational modes

In *Narration in the Fiction Film*, Bordwell defines a narrational mode as 'a historically distinct set of norms of narrational construction and comprehension'.[22] A mode is therefore a coherent and durable set of fundamental principles that circumscribe the norms for both filmmaking and film viewing and go beyond but also encompass other models of classification such as genre, movement, school or national cinema. Narrational modes are intrinsically tied to modes of film production and reception where norms are established through specific sets of practices and forms of industrial organisation. The identification of a dominant, historically specific narrational mode makes it possible, therefore, to analyse a film as within or deviating from established norms. Bordwell is quick to point out, however, that whilst a film may seem to be challenging the established narrational canon, 'within the reigning norm there is always a range of differentiation . . . A deviation from mainstream practice tends itself to be organized with respect to another extrinsic norm, however much a minority affair it may be'.[23] The matter of extrinsic and intrinsic norms is important here as intrinsic norms, the 'rules' established within the text often through repetition, may be dynamic and can change during a film to satisfy the extrinsic norms of the general narrational mode. In a detective mystery for instance the internal norm of communicativeness of the film – that is, the degree of knowledge shared by the narration – may alternate between being initially suppressed and subjective to being unrestricted. Such a deviation in intrinsic norms is thus important to the process of establishing and testing viewer expectations.[24]

The relationship between the viewer and the narrational mode is significant here, particularly when thinking about the recent surge in narrative complexity and how an audience makes sense of a film such as *Memento*. Edward Branigan (1992) argues that memory and inference are crucial to narrative comprehension as a spectator cannot remember every aspect of a film but instead relies on prior knowledge and experiences of the world and other films to produce a schema which classifies sensory data and is used to predict events.[25] From previous experiences of films the narrational norms come to constitute, in part, a schema which is then applied by the spectator. Expectations, inferences and hypothoses will be formed based on the film's adherence to or deviation from the intrinsic and extrinsic norms of the narrational mode. Narrative comprehension is thus a dynamic process that involves the viewer continually testing expectations and making inferences based on an applied schema, which in turn is partly composed from previous knowledge of extrinsic norms.

Classical narration, one of four narrational modes which Bordwell identifies, is 'a particular configuration of normalized options for representing the fabula and manipulating the possibilities of syuzhet and style'.[26] Using terms borrowed from Russian Formalist critics, Bordwell proposes that the fabula is the wider story which the viewer constructs from the *syuzhet*, the limited narrative material that appears on screen. Within classical narration, the *syuzhet* follows the canonic format of an initial state of affairs which is disrupted and eventually returned to a new or restored equilibrium; in short, a beginning, a middle and an end. The *syuzhet* is composed of sequences that are bounded by particular norms – for instance, a wipe, fade or sound bridge. A sequence is made up of scenes with distinct phases of exposition, character action, and the opening, suspension and closure of causal lines. Clear differentiation between scenes is signalled by duration, a definable location and cause–effect-based character action. In classical narrative it is causality that drives the forward linear momentum and the principal causal agent is a psychologically defined, goal-driven character, usually the protagonist, who must face some sort of obstacle or struggle to achieve, or fail to achieve, a particular resolution. Each scene advances the causal progression by continuing cause–effect developments from the previous scene. In this way, the end of one scene will leave a causal line open to be picked up in the following scene. In classical narration it is also common to have two plot-lines, a double causal structure. One plot-line will present a, usually heterosexual, romance, whilst the other will involve a different sphere of action, and often the two-plot lines will eventually coincide towards the end. The classical ending brings together the two causal lines via a string of events that lead logically from the initial cause to a final resolution. According to Bordwell, 'whether a protagonist learns a moral lesson or only the spectator knows the whole story, the classical film moves steadily toward a growing awareness of absolute truth'.[27]

The historical longevity of classical narrative demonstrates the stability of narrative structures and the dominant principles of storytelling which have been systematically developed and reiterated through a wealth of screenwriting manuals since the early decades of the twentieth century. Bordwell and Kristin Thompson argue that influential manuals which have popularised narrative principles, such as Syd Field's *Screenplay*, reiterate storytelling guidelines that had been in screenwriting handbooks since the early decades of the twentieth century.[28] They recount how, following the downsizing of the studios during the 1960s, screenwriters became freelance rather than studio contract workers. Without formal training, screenwriters turned to manuals and handbooks for guidance on screenplay conventions and by the early 1980s principles such as the three-act structure, cause-and-effect chains, turning points and goal-seeking protagonists that drive the main line of action had become widely recognised as the structural template for the narrative film.

The three-act structure promulgated through many screenwriting manuals is based on the Aristotelian formulation of a story that breaks down into temporal proportions of ¼–½–¼ with Act 1 of a 120 minute film ending at around page 30 of the screenplay. Act 2 lasts for around 60 pages and Act 3 approximately 30 pages, where each page equates to around one minute of screen time. The end of Act 1 and Act 2 are marked by a turning point or plot point, an event that moves the story in a different direction, and which is usually indicated by a shift in the protagonist's goals.[29] However, in her analysis of the structural model of narrative film, Thompson argues that the majority of films can be broken down into four, rather than three acts: with major turning points signalling the transition between the set-up, the complicating action, the development and the climax.[30] The set-up functions as exposition, the complicating action 'raises the emotional stakes', the development 'focuses attention on the steps the character must take to resolve their problems' whilst the climax presents the resolution.[31] Instead of the major turning points occurring only at the end of acts 1 and 2, there is a further major turning point in the middle of the majority of films. It is this turning point that marks out the four part structure that both Thompson and Bordwell consider to be a feature of classical narrative.

Despite the ubiquity of classical narrative, alternatives to this dominant narrational mode have always existed. Where classical narrative presents a tightly structured form of realism, a legacy of the clarity and unity of both narrative and individual identity in the nineteenth-century short story and popular novel, art cinema narration derives its realism from literary modernism where personal psychology and truth may be vague, imprecise or uncertain.[32] Causality is loosened and instead of having clear deadlines such as those imposed within classical narrative to drive the causal line forward, art cinema narration adopts a more open-ended approach that favours chance and causal gaps. This loose causality relies on a protagonist who does not display the well-defined character traits required by classical narrative and may instead be inconsistent in both their psychology and actions. Characters' mental states, feelings and various forms of subjectivity are expressed in both sound and image through devices such as flash frames and optical point-of-view shots. Expressive realism in art cinema narration is therefore motivated by character psychology and the differences between art cinema and classical narration translate into a differentiation of emphasis with art cinema foregrounding character over plot and classical narrative giving prominence to plot over character.[33]

The tight structure of classical cinema is eschewed in art cinema in favour of a looser relationship between scenes which do not necessarily follow the phases of exposition, character action and causal development. This looseness is realised in delayed exposition and causes which have no resolution or do not form part of a linear causal chain and lead to narrative ambiguity and open endings. Temporal manipulations, such as flashbacks and flashforwards, characteristic of art cinema narration, can also promote ambiguity and the viewer may be uncertain whether these devices represent dreams, fantasies or memories; it may also be difficult to determine how trustworthy such information is. Ambiguity is therefore absolutely central to art cinema narration. Bordwell expresses this when he writes: 'the syuzhet of classical narration tends to move toward absolute certainty, but the art film, like early modernist fiction, holds a relativistic notion of truth'.[34] Given the characteristics of this mode of narration and the particular emphasis on ambiguity, temporal reordering and subjective states, can *Memento* and other independent 'puzzle films' be adequately accounted for by art cinema or classical narration? Beyond speculating that a viewer will watch a puzzle film again to work out 'how it was done', the analysis that follows focuses on particular features of *Memento* that can be identified as 'repaying' the viewer for watching the film more than once. The aim here is not to disambiguate the narrative but to reveal the narrational mechanisms which produce such ambiguity.

Memento

The reverse colour title sequence, a series of fifteen shots, opens with a close-up of a Polaroid photograph which fades slowly over its 73-second duration. The second shot, another close-up, follows the Polaroid as it is sucked up into the camera, which flashes; the camera then moves down and out of frame to allow the shot to finish as a close-up of Leonard's face. The obvious reversal of events and action in the first two shots is accompanied by sound cues, most notably of the Polaroid coming out of the camera, and the music score, that run forward and therefore counter to what is seen. In the series of shots that follow, the temporal direction is less apparent. A close-up of Leonard's face, a bullet casing on the floor, a pair of spectacles and the back of Teddy's head lying on the blood-spattered floor do not have enough movement in them to suggest the retrogression of time. Only one shot of blood that seems to defy gravity and slides up a wall is at odds with what could be inferred as the normal forward progression of action and events. Viewers are then forced to revise any notion they may have about time progressing normally in shots 9–15 as the action runs in reverse; a gun flies from the ground into Leonard's hand, a bullet case rolls backwards and out of shot, a pair of spectacles fly into the air, Teddy's body rises from the floor, the bullet case goes back into the gun chamber, the gun is fired and Teddy's body spins round.

The foregrounding of stylistic devices in the title sequence draws attention to the relationship between film style, *syuzhet* and narrative comprehension. Motivational rationales applied by the viewer are cued and channelled by the interaction of *syuzhet* and style, and in the opening scene the stylistic features, which are expressly emphasised, increase the possible explanations that may be inferred. If the scene were presented according to the norms of temporal organisation and Leonard shot Teddy, then took a photograph of his dead body, the film's style could pass unnoticed leaving the viewer to apply compositional motivation to the sequence.[35] This would assume that it is relevant to the story and invite the viewer to speculate on the series of events that either precede or proceed from it. But in this case, the reversed action makes the film's stylistic choices prominent in the opening sequence.

One rationale for the reversed presentation could posit a justification of artistic motivation, whereby the stylistic device does not support the *syuzhet* but instead is there as a flourish in its own right. But, cognitive psychology suggests that a viewer will always attempt to construct a story even when confronted by seemingly inexplicable stylistic emphasis. It is possible therefore that the spectator could apply schemata that include previous experiences of, for instance, time travel or supernatural narratives to posit a realistic motivation that, on transtextual grounds, in the film world of *Memento* things can go backwards. Yet, interviews with the director confirm that the stylistic choices taken in the opening scene were intended to summarise the structure of the film for the audience. This presents an interesting situation, because the same device is not repeated in any subsequent scenes the reversed action quickly loses its significance. Delayed exposition and the complex nature of the causal chain force the viewer to become involved in trying to construct a coherent fabula, and comprehension of the *syuzhet* takes precedence over proposing a rationale for the foregrounding of style in the opening scene. In short, spectators are so taken up with making sense of the film it is possible that they quickly forget about the reversed action in the opening scene. Because the opening stylistic devices are subordinated early on, the opening scene is a good example of a feature of *Memento* that may function as part of the 'payback' for watching it again when the spectator arrives at a subsequent viewing with knowledge of the film's structure. In this sense, the opening scene makes apparent the dynamic relationship between film style, *syuzhet* and narrative comprehension. Artistically motivated stylistic choices create ambiguity by opening up possible hypotheses about motivational rationales, which in the case of *Memento* may be revealed and resolved when the film is watched a second time and can be proposed as part of the pleasure to be derived from multiple viewings.

The scene that follows introduces the second plot-line which immediately contrasts with the previous colour title sequence as it is shot in black and white. Such differentiation recalls traditional stylistic norms for the presentation of an alternative space, time, subjectivity or reality that have been used, for instance in *The Wizard of Oz* (Fleming, 1939), *A Matter of Life and Death* (Powell and Pressburger, 1946), *Schindler's List* (Spielberg, 1993), *Purple Rose of Cairo* (Allen, 1985) and *Natural Born Killers* (Stone, 1994). In this case, the brief second scene, which lasts only 21 seconds, introduces the stylistic devices that will recur throughout the film. The narrative information presented early in a film also gives the viewer a frame of reference against which hypotheses can be formed and revised. The privilege that an audience affords to the initial part of a film, the primacy effect, '"primes" us to label a person or situation using a type of schema which biases the way in which we interpret and attend to, subsequent information'.[36] It is significant, therefore, that in the second scene the killer, Leonard, from the opening title sequence is presented as confused and vulnerable, his vulnerability emphasised by his partially clad body, and the musical score reflecting his tense, even paranoid, mental state. The setting, a motel room, lacks any visual cues to help the audience infer much else about him. The dressing table is bare, the coathangers and closet area are empty and Leonard's voiceover reinforces the disorienting anonymity of the surroundings. With Leonard, the audience is looking for visual clues to make sense of the environment. Voiceover and two subjective shots of the motel room from Leonard's position on the bed initiate the restricted narration that will continue throughout the film. This limit to Leonard's range of knowledge is significant as systematic restriction forces audience identification with the protagonist, a point which becomes crucial when the audience is invited to judge the reliability of the narration later.

The next scene is again in colour and a close-up of a Polaroid of Teddy, the man killed in the opening scene. Although Bert, the motel attendant, is present and has some dialogue at the beginning of the third scene he is confined to the background of a medium shot of Leonard who, having been present in the first three scenes, is established as the primary agent of knowledge. Teddy appears at the motel entrance and by returning to a state of affairs where the character who died in the first scene now appears alive, the narration allows the audience to create a hypothesis about the temporal relationship between the first and third scenes and to assume that the narrative is now depicting events that have occurred prior to the shooting. The gap in information invites the viewer to consider the causal chain and creates curiosity about the events that might have transpired to lead Leonard to kill Teddy. In this scene, a long-term relationship between Teddy and Leonard is established with Teddy noting that Leonard talks about 'his condition' every time he sees him, and Teddy's reliability is brought into question as he attempts to deceive Leonard into taking the wrong car. Leonard holds up a photograph of his Jaguar car to 'prove' Teddy's deception and show that he is not easily fooled. A broken window in the car is not explained and is unquestioned by either Leonard or Teddy. Instead the narration emphasises Leonard's 'condition', 'handicap' and inability to remember why he needs to go to a derelict building. On their arrival there the narration establishes transtextual motivations whereby the norms of the detective story are clearly foregrounded. For instance, Leonard finds 'clues' such as fresh tyre marks and he examines the bullets he finds on the seat of a deserted station wagon.

On entering the deserted building, Leonard consults his photographs. Restricted to Leonard's knowledge, the audience can see what is written about Teddy on the back of one image: 'Don't believe his lies. He is the one. Kill him'. The interior monologue reinforces identification with Leonard, as he and audience discover information at the same time. Assuming a subjective and highly communicative mode, the voiceover gives the viewer access to Leonard's thoughts and to the rationale that leads him to kill Teddy. This information fills gaps in the fabula as a causal relationship is now established between the events in this scene and the shooting in the first scene. Leonard's killing of Teddy is now justified and may be understood through realistic and transtextual motivations; Leonard is established via classical norms as goal-oriented, and in the revenge narrative killing is 'what the protagonist does'. Hints that Teddy is not to be trusted from the earlier part of the colour sequence are confirmed by what is written on the back of the Polaroid and this delimits the possible schemata that can be applied to him; Teddy is confirmed as untrustworthy.

The exchange between Teddy and Leonard that occurs immediately prior to the shooting closes down another gap as the revenge hypothesis is reasserted by Lenny's insistence that Teddy beg for his wife's forgiveness. But gaps are opened through Teddy's dialogue. He asserts that Leonard doesn't know what is going on, doesn't know Teddy's real name, doesn't know who or what he has become and that there is evidence in the basement which will prove that all this is true. The dialogue flaunts what is not known and creates suspense about how these questions will be answered by the *syuzhet* but, because Teddy has been established as unreliable, the questions also create a diffuse gap that is open to multiple inferences. One hypothesis that relies on realistic motivation provided by the information that both Leonard and the audience have is that Teddy is lying to buy time or to talk his way out of being killed. However, because of the restricted narration and Leonard's condition Teddy can know more than Leonard, which undermines the definitive status of the information that the narration has given up to this point. Leonard then

Figure 1 Restricted to Leonard's knowledge, the audience can see what is written about Teddy on the back of the Polaroid (© Newmarket / I Remember Productions)

kills Teddy and a temporal relationship between two scenes is created as the shooting makes it apparent that this scene has constituted the events immediately preceding Teddy's death in the opening scene.

By the end of the second colour sequence there has been limited exposition and the *syuzhet* has opened up diffuse and flaunted gaps in the fabula. The restricted narration establishes Leonard as the main agent of knowledge which channels audience identification with him. Whilst a causal line is established for Teddy's killing, the *syuzhet* complicates classical norms by reordering events into an effect–cause rather than cause–effect relationship. The second black and white scene introduces Sammy Jankis and the tattoo 'Remember Sammy Jankis' on Leonard's hand. This opens up a gap which is then left dangling to be picked up later; who is Sammy Jankis and why does Leonard need to remember him? This scene also begins to address the exposition as the voiceover, which reveals a high level of narrational self-consciousness, explains more about Leonard's condition, his experience of living with it and his use of a 'system'. A medium shot of a note taped to the top of Leonard's leg with the word 'Shave' on it closes the second black and white scene and functions to give more information about Leonard's 'system'. This becomes a dialogue hook into the next colour scene which opens with a close-up of someone writing 'Kill him' on the back of Teddy's photograph. The next shot cuts to Leonard loading a gun, which verifies that he has written the note and that photographs and notes are part of the system he has referred to.

The structure of alternating colour and black and white scenes is apparent by the third colour sequence, which also demonstrates the high level of redundancy in *Memento*. Redundancy, which in film studies refers to repetition that reinforces important information, is absolutely crucial in *Memento* due to its complicated structure. Visual and sonic cues are repeated to orient the spectator within the temporally reorganised narration. At the opening of the third colour sequence the close-up of the reverse of Teddy's photograph not only gives the viewer information about who wrote 'Kill him' and therefore diminishes the possible hypothesis that Leonard's activities are being directed by someone else, but also provides a temporal cue. Witnessing the writing of the note, the viewer can infer that this event must have taken place before Teddy is shot in the derelict building and at this point the reverse structure of the colour sequences is apparent. The spectator is now alerted again to the issue of Leonard's memory condition as, despite having written the note at some point before the shooting, Leonard was not able to remember it. The Polaroid of Teddy has now been present in the first three colour sequences and this redundancy functions as a signpost for the audience, crucial to viewer orientation within the narration and for establishing temporal and causal relationships.[37]

Clearly agitated, Leonard leaves his motel room during the third colour sequence and the level of narrational communicativeness increases as the camera follows his urgent walk. Information about the motel, the spatial relationship between the room and the reception desk and Leonard's room number are communicated in four shots. On arriving, Leonard's announces his name and room number to open a conversation with Bert, the motel desk clerk. Unsure whether he has asked Bert to hold his phone calls or not, the exchange between them that follows gives the viewer a detailed explanation of his condition. During Leonard's description of his short-term memory loss, now revealed to be the outcome of an injury, it becomes clear that Bert is only pretending not to have heard the story before and, despite his claim, 'I mean, I don't mean to mess with you, but it's so weird', the narration suggests that he is potentially untrustworthy.

This exchange between Leonard and Bert in this scene is significant as it includes references to the film's structure and stylistic choices that may not be apparent on first viewing. When asked what his condition 'is like', Leonard replies, 'It's like waking, it's like you just woke up'. Bert responds, 'That must suck. It's all backwards. I mean, like maybe you get an idea about what you wanna do next but you don't remember what you just did', offering a reference to the inverted narrative and effect–cause structure. However, as the references are contained within dialogue, which in classical narrative tends to be less self-conscious than voiceover for instance, it is reasonable to assume that audiences are not cued for information about the film structure through this manner of address. On a second viewing, however, the narrational self-consciousness of the scene is elevated. As the viewer does not have to process the information about Leonard's short-term memory condition contained in the dialogue and instead is cued to look for other subtle references, the allusions to narrative structure display a self-conscious recognition of the audience, in effect pointing out to the viewer how the film is constructed. Such references to structure are littered throughout the film and point to elevated narrational self-consciousness of particular scenes on a second viewing which are clearly a significant aspect of the multiple viewing pleasures of a puzzle film such as *Memento*.

The third colour sequence ends by repeating shots from the beginning of the second colour sequence: a close-up of the Polaroid of Teddy with sonic cues from Bert tapping his finger on the photograph, a close-up of Leonard turning to look towards the motel door, which cuts to a wide pan left to Teddy standing at the door, again with repeated sonic cues of his two raps on the glass and then cuts to a medium shot of Teddy exclaiming 'Lenny!' The repetition of enacted events which continues throughout the film is unusual even for classical narratives, which tend to have a high level of redundancy. Although an event may be recounted multiple times through dialogue it is usually enacted only once unless motivated by a flashback.[38] However, *Memento*'s reversed plot-line and consequent episodic structure rely on the repetition of enacted events to anchor the viewer within the narrative, so redundancy of repeated visual and sonic cues is crucial to narrative comprehension. The third black and white sequence also utilises redundancy in this way as it begins by returning to the final shot of the previous black and white sequence, a medium shot of a note taped to Leonard's leg with the word 'Shave' written on it and continues the action with Leonard's voiceover stating; 'You really need a system if you're gonna make it work.'

The voiceover in the third black and white sequence is ambiguous as it has a high degree of self-consciousness but is not presented as enacted recounting.[39] It is clear that the voiceover is not describing internal thought processes that are occurring simultaneously with the presented action but instead that Leonard's description of his 'system' is addressed to someone not apparent to the viewer and therefore can be assumed to be taking place at another time. Although it is unclear at this point whom Leonard is addressing, the loose, relaxed style of the voiceover, coupled with the black and white photography, draws on transtextual references to documentary film which emphasise the reliability of the information being presented.[40] Talking about trusting only his own writing closes down possible hypotheses that Leonard can be easily duped even though he suggests that people will try to take advantage of him. A reference to writing important notes on the body is accompanied by a shot of Leonard peering down his shirt to his chest which opens up a gap in information. Leonard has seen something on his skin that the narration does not allow the viewer access to. The sound of a phone ringing halts Leonard's investigation of his body as he turns his attention to the phone, thereby eliminating the possibility that the spectator will be offered a point of view shot of his chest. With the interruption the voiceover stops and Leonard's anxious question 'Who is this?' to an unknown caller opens up a gap that is left dangling.

The fourth colour sequence begins with Leonard in a bathroom washing his hands. A close-up of his left hand accompanied by his voiceover reading the tattoo 'Remember Sammy Jankis' repeats the reference to Sammy made in the second black and white sequence. Subjective close-ups allow the viewer to begin to discover the tattoos on Leonard's body as he pulls back his sleeve to reveal one which reads 'The facts'. Someone entering the bathroom interrupts the investigation of Leonard's body for a second time, flaunting the curiosity gap opened in the previous scene. A quick cut from a subjective close-up to a more objective medium shot emphasises the surprise caused by the unexpected interruption. Leonard leaves the bathroom and an optical point of view shot, married with the stylistic choice of handheld camerawork, reveals that he is in a diner. An employee hands Leonard a brown envelope and a motel key which are partly obscured by Leonard's hand and a Polaroid of the motel sign. Leonard asks for directions to Lincoln Street then drives to the Discount Inn.

In his motel room the narration once again shifts to a higher level of self-consciousness as Leonard sticks Polaroids onto a makeshift relational map pinned to the wall whilst the voiceover reiterates the key information that the spectator needs to remember: 'Discount Inn', 'My car' and 'Teddy'. This part of the scene also introduces a new name, Natalie, with an ambiguous Polaroid image of a partially silhouetted figure. What is significant is the order in which the information is presented – Teddy is the final Polaroid that Leonard sticks to the map. A wide shot of Leonard opening the brown envelope is followed by a close-up to reveal its contents, a photocopy of Teddy's driver licence, and the writing on the envelope, 'For Leonard from Natalie'. Cutting to another close-up of the licence, Leonard's internal voiceover reads the name on it, 'John Edward Gammell', and articulates the knowledge gap that he and the viewer now share: the question of Teddy's true identity. The narration is both restricted and highly communicative as the audience is given access to Leonard's thoughts and discoveries as he makes them, further reinforcing spectator identification with him. Leonard turns Teddy's Polaroid over to reveal the note 'Don't believe his lies'. He calls the phone number written on the front of Teddy's photograph and whilst he waits for Teddy to arrive at the motel room he continues with the investigation of his body which has been twice interrupted.

With Leonard, the spectator discovers the various tattoos that cover his body as he undresses. Medium, close-up and point of view shots fragment Leonard's body into readable tattooed statements which align the spectator's knowledge with Leonard's sense of being in the world and advisory messages alert the viewer to the problematic status of information and memory: 'Photograph; House; Car; Friend; Foe', 'Don't trust', 'Notes can be lost', 'Consider the source', Memory is treachery'. After establishing the unreliable nature of remembered information the next set of tattoos reveal a series of 'facts' which are reinforced by Leonard's reading them out loud. At the same time, the narration positions the 'facts' as clues and relates each to the information about Teddy/John Gammell that has been supplied in the brown envelope. As Leonard repeats the 'facts' he elects to read to himself only part of the Fact 3 tattoo, 'First name John', and ignores the second part of the inscription, 'or James', which is clearly a later and more amateurish addition. As Leonard's articulation of written information as voiceover has been established during the earlier scenes as a way to highlight the salient information for the spectator, his omission opens up the hypotheses that 'or James' is not important and therefore can be discarded at this

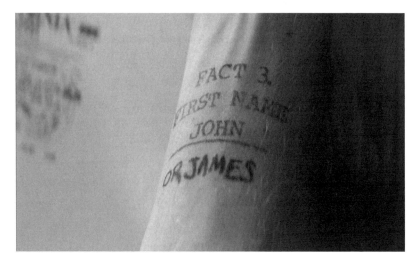

Figure 2 As Leonard repeats the 'facts', he ignores the second part of the inscription (© Newmarket / I Remember Productions)

stage of the narrative as well as the possibility that Leonard is able to ignore certain facts and be selective about the information he chooses to assimilate.[41] The correlation between the licence plate number and the tattoo of Fact 6 and the trans-textual references to the detective/revenge narrative provide the motivation for murdering Teddy. Believing he has discovered that Teddy is John G. Leonard writes 'He is the one' on the back of Teddy's Polaroid, then catches sight of the tattoo 'John G raped and murdered my wife' written backwards on his chest thereby establishing a causal link that motivates him to add 'Kill him' to the reverse of the photo and returns the spectator to the first two shots of the previous colour sequence – the close-up of Leonard writing the note, followed by a medium shot of Leonard loading his gun.

The fifth black and white sequence makes apparent the changing registers of communicativeness that the narration assumes. In this sequence, Leonard continues his conversation with the unknown caller on the telephone which had ended the previous black and white scene. In the colour scene that immediately preceded, the viewer is able to hear Leonard's telephone conversation and so establish with him that he is speaking to Teddy, thereby confirming Teddy's identity deception. The caller's identity during the telephone conversation that continues in the fifth black and white sequence is withheld by adopting a less communicative, more objective narrational stance so that the spectator is no longer given access to everything that Leonard sees and hears. Realistic motivation would also cue the spectator to hypothesise that given Leonard's condition he would be unable to remember a person's voice, which flaunts the gap about the speaker's identity and heightens curiosity whilst opening up an avenue of exposition where Leonard can recount the Sammy Jankis story. This short scene, which last a little over 40 seconds, again achieves a high level of redundancy in an effort to confirm the revenge trajectory of the narrative. This is achieved by foregrounding Leonard's 'Kill him' and 'John G. raped and murdered my wife' tattoos within six shots and ending the scene with Leonard's statement that he has a reason to maintain a rigorous, methodical 'system' as he re-reads the latter tattoo in the mirror. Manipulation of the fabula by the *syuzhet* during this scene and the previous colour scene cues the spectator to recognise Teddy as the guilty suspect and provides a realistic motivation for Leonard's investigation and revenge. With Teddy's guilt confirmed, two main gaps are opened by the narration, the question of why Teddy killed Leonard's wife and what the cause–effect chain was that brought Leonard to the revelatory moment where he identifies the killer.

Bordwell suggests that in the detective film such gaps are usually flaunted so that

> The viewer creates a set of exclusive hypotheses – a closed set of suspects, a gradually defined range of outcomes. The genre promotes suspense with respect to the twists and turns of the investigation and plays upon curiosity about the missing causal material.[42]

Assuming classical norms, the reverse structure makes revealing Teddy as the killer at this point in the narrative highly plausible. Working backwards from the point where the investigation has apparently ended and the guilty party exposed, the spectator is channelled towards an expectation that the *syuzhet* will now be committed to revealing the events that occurred prior to Leonard's discovery of Teddy as the killer, with a possible but limited hypothesis that suggests from transtextual experience that a suspect identified early in a detective narrative may turn out to be a red herring.

In the fifth colour scene, Leonard arrives outside a diner to meet Natalie. The second shot, a close-up of the arrangements for the meeting scribbled on a paper bag and the photograph of Natalie with the note

'She has also lost someone. She will help you out of pity', are recounted by Leonard's interior monologue, access to his thoughts now having been established as an intrinsic norm. Although visible a crossed-out line of writing on the back of Natalie's Polaroid is not emphasised. The narration shifts from a highly communicative register to a restricted shot of Leonard as he walks into the diner, allowing him to observe the environment before the spectator does. A wide shot from behind Leonard moves the narration into a self-conscious mode which shifts to a less self-conscious register as Leonard is identified by Natalie and a dialogue exchange foregrounds Leonard's condition and wife again. Natalie's attempt to goad Leonard by knowingly calling him Lenny, a name he hates, and the undercurrent of antipathy apparent when she refers to his notes and 'freaky tattoos' opens a gap by being at odds with the idea that Natalie pities him. At the same time her comments establish that she has detailed knowledge of Leonard's body, suggesting intimacy between them. Natalie offers Leonard the brown envelope, reminding him that he gave her the licence plate number which a friend of hers at DMV was able to trace, a point which adds credence to the robust nature of the information chain. Moreover Natalie, having had sight of the driver licence picture of Teddy/John G., asserts that she does not know him but that he may have been in the bar. The question of whether taking revenge for something that Leonard cannot remember is worthwhile is raised by Natalie, who then encourages him to remember his wife, motivating the narration to shift to a flashback. Natalie admonishes Leonard for 'just reciting words' when he attempts to describe his wife as beautiful and perfect, forcing him to close his eyes to 'remember her'. The external flashback,[43] differentiated by the use of loose, hand-held camerawork from the colour sequence in the diner, is therefore motivated by Leonard's recollection. A montage of thirteen shots of Leonard's wife reflects his assertion that when remembering, 'You can just feel the details. The bits and pieces you never bothered to put into words. . . . You put these together and you get the feel of a person.' When the flashback ends Natalie tells Leonard that she has also provided him with the address of an abandoned place out of town and that she was not helping him for money. After giving him his motel key which she says he left at her place, Natalie claims that they are both survivors then leaves. Leonard gets up and goes to the bathroom where the shot of him washing his hands and the close-up of the Sammy Jankis tattoo from the beginning of the fourth colour sequence end this colour scene with the dialogue hook 'Remember Sammy Jankis', which is then picked up in the following black and white sequence as Leonard continues his telephone conversation with the unknown caller.

The fifth black and white sequence establishes that Leonard's job as an insurance investigator led to his relationship with Sammy Jankis, something he refers to as his first 'real challenge'. Leonard's explanation that he has to look into someone's eyes to 'figure them out' repeats information and clarifies an event that has occurred in the previous colour sequence when he asks Natalie to remove her sunglasses. A black and white flashback motivated by Leonard's recounting of his experiences as an insurance investigator and differentiated from the black and white motel room shots primarily by the even lighting is simultaneously re-enacted with shots of various unidentified individuals displaying the characteristics and micro-expressions that Leonard relies on to determine whether people are reliable or not.

The sixth colour sequence reintroduces Teddy. During lunch together an exchange between Leonard and Teddy offers a further opportunity to recount his main goal: to find John G. The narration foregrounds questions about the reliability of memory, notes, pictures and facts in their discussion, and Teddy introduces a new complication with the assertion that Leonard has previously been concerned that he is being set up to kill the wrong person. As the narration has striven during the previous scenes to establish Teddy as unreliable the spectator is channelled to regard all of his statements with caution and as potentially untrustworthy. In a defence of his revenge goal, Leonard clarifies the relationship between his memory condition and his wife's rape and murder, claiming that John G. is responsible for both.

Realising that his motel key is missing, Leonard returns to the Discount Inn where Bert unlocks a room for him. Objects related to shaving which have been repeatedly visible in previous black and white sequences (shaving foam, razors, an ice bucket and paper bag) are strewn across the bed. When Bert says that he has brought Leonard to the wrong room, the spectator and Leonard are cued to pick up the deception at the same time. A close-up shot of a white paper bag with the words 'Shave left thigh' in Leonard's handwriting, which has been emphasised as a close-up in an earlier black and white scene offers proof that he has been in this room and also locates the black and white sequences as occurring prior to the current colour sequence. A specific temporal relationship between the black and white and colour scenes is established when Bert admits that the room was rented to Leonard the previous week until Bert had been encouraged by the motel owner to rent him another room, room 304. The black and white sequences are now established as occurring a week prior to the events presented in colour. Bert's suggestion that such a deception can be avoided in the future by always getting a receipt prompts Leonard to reach into his pocket for a pen and paper where he discovers the note with the details of his meeting with Natalie. Leonard rushes off to meet her and the sequence ends with the repeated wide shot of his Jaguar car pulling up to the kerb, followed by the wide shot from behind Leonard in the diner, a close-up reaction shot of Leonard's face in response to Natalie grabbing the back of his jacket and a shot of Natalie which are shots 1, 6, 7 and 8 from colour sequence 5. The narrational gap created by leaving out shots 2–5 at the end of the sixth colour sequence suggests that the spectator is expected to understand the structure of the film at this stage and that the omitted shots are unnecessary redundancy.

A close-up of Leonard shaving his right thigh is the first shot of the sixth black and white sequence which provides further confirmation of the temporal relationship between this and the colour plot-line. The razor, ice bucket and the shaving foam on Leonard's leg are visual cues to prompt the audience to make the link back to the same objects strewn across the bed, which Leonard now sits on, from the previous colour sequence. A flashback is used to present the events related to Sammy Jankis, On the phone to the unknown caller, Leonard's voiceover recounts the enacted events of Sammy's diagnosis and Leonard's arrival at the Jankis' house to investigate their insurance claim. Sammy's ability to undertake complex tasks that he learnt before his accident is presented in six close-ups of him giving his wife an insulin injection. The flashback is followed by a close-up of Leonard in the motel room telling the unknown caller that his suspicion about Sammy's condition led him to call for further tests, a causal line that is picked up in the next black and white scene.

The seventh colour sequence begins with a close-up of Leonard's face. Two scratch marks which have been visible throughout the colour scenes are emphasised as the voiceover articulates Leonard's thought process and the spectator discovers a new environment shot by shot along with him. The highly restricted narration discloses only minor details of the room one at a time; shots of bird cages, the top of a door and a two-shot of Leonard in bed with an unidentified woman, her back turned towards the camera. The woman is revealed to be Natalie and a shot of Leonard with his trousers on as he gets out of bed suggests that the two have not had sex. However, Natalie reminds Leonard of the tattoo on his thigh, which renders their level of intimacy less certain. Leonard reads the back of Natalie's Polaroid recounting the information again and a close-up of the reverse of the image offers a further reminder that part of the original note has been scribbled out. After getting out of bed Natalie writes down on a paper bag where and when Leonard is to meet her and states that she is helping him because he once helped her. Natalie's expectation that Leonard will remember her when they next meet offers some motivation for her antipathy toward him in the diner in the earlier fifth colour sequence. Leonard leaves Natalie's house and a sound overlap of the car engine starting then cuts to a shot of Leonard in his car, followed by a medium shot of Teddy leaping on the bonnet of the car are the first two shots of colour sequence six.

Continuing Leonard's recounting of the Sammy Jankis story, the seventh black and white sequence includes a flashback of Sammy's memory being tested with electrified objects. Deep staging in the second shot of the flashback shows Leonard in the background watching Sammy's test through a window whilst the tester, in the foreground, instructs Sammy to pick up any three objects on the table in front of him. Lasting only 45 seconds, this black and white scene ends with Leonard's remarking that the purpose of the test is to see if Sammy can learn to avoid the electrified objects by instinct rather than memory.

A sense of urgency is suggested by the musical score that accompanies the first shot of the eighth colour sequence – a wide shot of Leonard's car arriving at Natalie's house – which also communicates the passage of time with the setting now at dusk. Within the norms of the three-act structure, Leonard's demand that Natalie tell him who Dodd is and the close-up of a Polaroid of a man with his mouth taped and a bloodied face constitute a major turning point and signal the shift towards the end of the first act.[44] Leonard is now implicated in another violent action, this time concerning Dodd, whose name is written on the front of the Polaroid. Natalie asserts that Leonard offered to go after Dodd to help her and as a reprisal for her own facial injuries, which she points out to Leonard. The causal chain seems to be logical given that references to their reciprocated help have been reiterated in previous scenes. However, Leonard vehemently disputes the causal chain and the instinct that he has mentioned in the previous black and white sequence is now brought to bear on these events as he claims, 'Something doesn't feel right. I think someone's fucking with me, trying to get me to kill the wrong guy.' This forces a re-evaluation of information to this point since, if someone is indeed trying to deceive Leonard for their own purposes, then Teddy's statement in the sixth colour sequence – that Leonard had told him he thought he was being setup – could be true. At this point the narration opens up a number of possible hypotheses with regard to who is trying to deceive him and, Teddy's ever dubious role, and the new question of Dodd's identity and significance in the chain of events is centralised.

The narration draws attention to questions about what is true and certain in an exchange between Leonard and Natalie, who then discovers his tattoos and removes his shirt to read the backward tattoo, 'John G. raped and killed my wife'. Asking about the area of his chest without tattoos, Leonard responds that the space over his heart is for when he finds John G. A photograph of Natalie with a man, Jimmy, is revealed to be the person she has lost when he did not return from a meeting with Teddy. Natalie's offer to help Leonard find John G. is now suspicious as the audience knows that John G. and Teddy are the same person and that Leonard has just said that he will kill John G. when he finds him. This raises the question of how much Natalie actually knows and whether her motivation to help Leonard is a fair exchange of assistance or part of a larger manipulation to set Leonard up to kill the man who may have killed Jimmy. Natalie, Teddy and Bert are now all potentially involved in manipulating Leonard for personal gain and whilst the narration had closed down the range of possible suspects guilty of killing Leonard's wife by the end of the fourth colour sequence, the end of act 1 opens up a new range of possible hypotheses about who can be trusted.

After a medium shot of Leonard and Natalie in bed together later that night, Leonard leaves the bedroom and in the living room looks at the photograph of Natalie and Jimmy. A shot of Natalie still in the bedroom caressing the bed where Leonard has been lying shifts the narration from being restricted to Leonard's experience, and the audience is given access to information that is unavailable to him. Returning to a shot of Leonard in the living room the audience witnesses Leonard writing the note about Natalie on the reverse of her Polaroid. A cut to a second shot of Natalie in bed is followed by a close-up of Natalie's Polaroid note and Leonard's interior monologue recounting what he has written. He returns to the bed and the final shot of the eighth colour sequence, in a departure from what has been established as an intrinsic norm, does not repeat the opening action or events from the seventh colour sequence. The eighth black and white sequence then progresses Leonard's recounting of the Sammy Jankis story and ends with the revelation that, as a result of Leonard's investigation and on the grounds that the condition was a 'mental illness', the insurance company was able to reject Sammy's claim. Leonard's summary of events, explaining that the company promoted him and left Mrs Jankis to deal with the mounting medical bills, marks the major turning point in the black and white plot-line.

Act 2 begins with a montage; first, light beneath a door, then a close-up of a woman's face beneath plastic which lasts only a few frames, the silhouette of someone approaching the door, the face beneath the plastic shower curtain, a white tiled floor with a piece of plastic in the bottom right of the frame, an extreme close-up of a woman's mouth gasping beneath the plastic, the light beneath the door, three further shots, lasting only a few frames, of plastic, a masked man, the woman beneath the plastic followed by Leonard being slammed against a bathroom mirror and a jar of blue bath crystals smashing on the floor. Leonard wakes suddenly, which invites the audience to hypothesise that the preceding shots were a dream (or nightmare) that has recalled events from the night when his wife was attacked. This dream signals the shift in the middle act towards diffuse gaps and indeterminacy where ambiguity is introduced into Leonard's recollections. At this point the audience has no reason to question the narration, despite the fact that psychologically motivated flashbacks tend to have a high degree of veracity within classical narrative as opposed to the dream sequence which tends to be less trustworthy. In the middle act the two become entwined and the reliability of Leonard's recollections is gradually eroded until, in the final act, his memories are unreliable.

The audience is channelled to recognise the familiarity of Leonard's predicament when, after waking from the nightmare and unable to remember where he is, he repeats his commentary about trying to find reference points in anonymous motel rooms from the first black and white scene of the film. This time, the drawers in the room contain the expected Gideon bible and, to Leonard's surprise, a gun. He goes to the closet which was empty in the first black and white scene only to find Dodd there, his mouth taped and bloodied. Knocking from outside causes Leonard to hurriedly close the closet door and a point of view shot through the peephole in the motel room door reveals Teddy outside peering back. Dodd confirms that Leonard has beaten him and Leonard and Teddy hatch a plan to get Dodd out of the room and force him to leave town. Leonard looks at the photograph of Dodd with 'Get rid of him. Ask Natalie' written on the reverse and although Natalie's Polaroid is partly visible underneath Dodd's picture Leonard declines to let Teddy see the image. In a two-shot, Leonard holds the photographs beyond the bottom of the frame out of sight of both Teddy and the audience. Leonard's eyeline suggests that he continues to look at the images, but the narration does not return to the photographs and the audience is left to speculate about what Leonard is looking at and why he resists Teddy's demands to see the image of Natalie. In what remains of the scene Teddy makes two failed attempts to acquire the Jaguar car and after Dodd has driven away, presumably leaving town for good, Leonard goes to Natalie's house to find out what is going on. The final four shots of the scene repeat shots 1, 3, 4 and 5 from the beginning of the eighth colour sequence and re-establish the instrinsic norm of redundancy from the first act.[45]

The ninth black and white sequence reopens the Sammy Jankis story through a flashback as Leonard continues his telephone conversation with the unknown caller. At this point the narration establishes the problems faced by Mr and Mrs Jankis due to Sammy's condition whilst following Leonard's preparations to tattoo his own leg. The next colour sequence begins with Leonard sitting on a toilet fully clothed with a bottle of alcohol in his hands. Momentary access to his thought processes establishes that he doesn't feel drunk but the narration then moves to a less communicative register and the voiceover ends. After looking in the mirror at the scratches on his face and undressing, a montage sequence reduces Leonard's showering to six shots until the sound of a door closing interrupts the ellipsis. Leonard is discovered in the shower by Dodd and a fight ensues which ends when Leonard hits Dodd across the head with the bottle, knocking him unconscious. Leonard conceals Dodd in the closet and photographs him. After dressing, Leonard finds a handwritten note about Dodd. Much of it is ignored and Leonard writes a selective summary of the information on the reverse of the Polaroid: 'Dodd. Get rid of him. Ask Natalie'. Leonard phones Teddy and leaves a message asking for his help, puts Dodd's gun in the drawer on top of the Gideon bible and waits for Teddy. By the end of the sequence the narration has established a causal relationship with the events in the preceding colour sequence. Now the audience knows how Dodd got in the closet and the gun was found in the drawer. In a change to the established norms of the narration, the end of the scene does not loop back to repeat any of the shots from the dream/nightmare sequence which opened the second act, but instead finishes with Leonard sitting on the bed.

In the tenth black and white sequence the phone conversation between Leonard and the unknown caller ends, allowing the narration to focus on Leonard's construction of a homemade tattooing tool made from a pen and needle. Working without instructions Leonard's ability to undertake such a complex task recalls Sammy Jankis preparing to inject his wife with insulin in an earlier scene, a parallel that is more apparent on a second viewing. In the final shot of the sequence Leonard snaps a pen in half and there is a cut to a colour shot of him running. Unlike the fade to or fade up from black transitions which have signalled the end of previous sequences the cut between these two scenes is abrupt. Leonard is being chased by Dodd but manages to escape and get to his car. Finding the note with Dodd's details, Leonard decides to wait for him in his motel room, where he selects a weapon (a bottle of alcohol). He then sits on the toilet to wait, with the final shot of the scene repeating shots 1 and 2 of the tenth colour sequence. The narration returns to a black and white scene as Leonard prepares to tattoo himself with Fact 5 ('Access to drugs') and this is followed by the twelfth colour sequence, which begins with Leonard out of doors beside a dying fire. Driving back to town Leonard is followed by a car, which turns out to be Dodd's. Dodd shatters Leonard's car window as he attempts to shoot Leonard who escapes and the scene ends with a repeat of the first shot of the eleventh colour sequence and the voiceover commentary that accompanied the third shot. The next black and white sequence continues to present Leonard about to tattoo his thigh when he is interrupted by the phone ringing. His question 'Who is this?' is not answered for the audience as the caller's identity is again withheld.

In the thirteenth colour sequence Leonard drives to a deserted industrial site where he builds a fire. Here, he attempts to forget his wife by burning her belongings and this motivates further flashbacks in the narration – recollections of his wife using the objects, which he then throws on the fire. In one flashback Leonard pinches his wife on the top of her thigh as she brushes her hair. He pulls some hair from the brush and burns it. In another flashback he questions why his wife would want to re-read a book. He smells the pages of the book and burns this along with a clock and a teddy bear. A dissolve indicates the passage of night into morning, suggesting that Leonard has sat by the fire all night.

The thirteenth black and white sequence returns to Leonard's telephone conversation with the unknown caller. Close-up shots of Leonard's file, an amalgamation of his handwritten notes and a police file, are opportunities for the spectator to pause and study at length on DVD the details which are on screen for only a few tantalising moments. For instance, a close-up of a partly covered piece of paper headed with the words 'Psychiatric Report' is never explained by the narration, opening up possible hypotheses about whom it refers to. Leonard explains that he acquired the file from a friend in the police force and that the police were not looking for John G. Pages that are missing and sentences and words crossed out in the various reports are highlighted in the narration both in Leonard's dialogue and through close-ups of the papers. This opens up a gap which becomes crucial later when the audience has to decide whether Leonard has intentionally sabotaged the file or whether there is another plausible explanation for the missing information. Treating *Memento* as a 'DVD-enabled film' – that is, having elements that re-pay viewing on DVD format – what becomes important about this sequence is that it provides further cues for the spectator to create hypotheses about Leonard's reliability, the close-up of the unidentified psychiatric report being a case in point.

Colour sequence 14 develops the disorientation of the narration through a series of shots that begin with Leonard waking. Subjective close-ups of objects that have been burned in the earlier sequence open up possible hyopotheses about where this scene is located within the fabula time-line. Leonard's tattoos indicate that the scene is taking place after his wife's attack but the possessions that the spectator has seen being burnt in the previous colour sequence are there, and Leonard calling to his wife as he wakes up make the temporal location of the scene uncertain. Shots repeated from the dream/nightmare sequence at the beginning of act 2 are ambiguous in this scene. It is unclear whether close-ups of his wife struggling, the white tiled bathroom floor and a masked attacker are occurring in parallel with Leonard waking and walking to the bathroom door, or whether the images are memories or dreams. Leonard presses his ear to the door, inferring that the audience is being given access to what he can hear on the other side. Leonard opens the door to reveal an unidentified woman snorting cocaine, which forces the spectator to re-evaluate the preceding shots as flashbacks. Leonard asks her to leave and the final shot of the sequence repeats the first two shots from colour sequence 13. In black and white sequence 14, the narration suppresses knowledge to such an extent that only Leonard has access to a

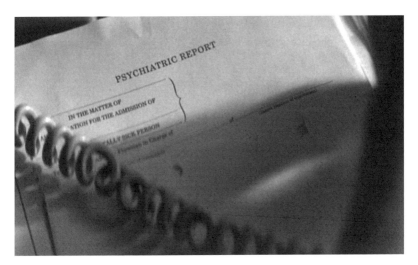

Figure 3 The 'psychiatric report' is never explained by the narration
(© Newmarket / I Remember Productions)

piece of information from his telephone conversation which he evaluates as so significant that he changes one of his facts, 'Access to drugs', and replaces it with 'Drug dealer'. With the identity of the caller still withheld, the spectator has no opportunity to judge the veracity of the information Leonard is being given.

In colour sequence 15, Leonard arrives at the Discount Inn. After taking a Polaroid of the motel sign, he parks his car, pins his hand-drawn map on the wall in the motel room and then phones for an escort. In this scene the unidentified woman in the bathroom is now established as the escort Leonard has hired and the events leading to Leonard waking and finding her are explained. Leonard has orchestrated the scenario asking the escort to place the objects around the room and when he is asleep to go to the bathroom and slam the door loud enough to wake him. The *syuzhet* presents these events, and in the final shot of the scene there is another occurrence when the audience has fleeting access to information unavailable to Leonard because he is asleep, when the escort gets out of bed. The narration does not follow her, however, and the shot stays on Leonard sleeping until the repeated sound cue of the bathroom door being slammed signals the end to the scene. In black and white sequence 15, Leonard has committed the fact 'Drug dealer' to his body as a tattoo. The narration foregrounds the problematic nature of the condition that Leonard and Sammy share in the flashback of Mrs Jankis's visit to Leonard's office to find out whether he believes Sammy to be faking or whether his condition is real. Leonard admits that he told Mrs Jankis that Sammy should be able to make new memories.

The colour sequence that follows opens with Leonard walking away from Natalie's house to his car where Teddy surprises him. Leonard responds by attacking him. In an exchange between them, Natalie's honesty is questioned and Teddy suggests that Leonard is being manipulated by her. He tells Leonard that Natalie's boyfriend is a drug dealer and that somebody will be going after Natalie because they will want to know what has happened to her boyfriend. Teddy claims that Natalie does not know who he is and forces Leonard to write 'Do not trust her' on the back of Natalie's Polaroid. Teddy repeats the claims from the early scene: Leonard does not know who or what he has become since the 'incident' and that he should investigate himself. Leonard dismisses Teddy's suggestions and after Teddy leaves the car Leonard considers what is written on the reverse of Teddy's and Natalie's photographs: 'Don't trust her' and 'Don't believe his lies'. Faced with the option that both Teddy and Natalie are untrustworthy, Leonard scribbles out 'Don't trust her' on the back of Natalie's photograph, an event that reinforces the hypothesis that it is Teddy who is the more untrustworthy. The sequence ends with a repeat shot of Leonard taking a photograph of the Discount Inn sign from the beginning of the previous sequence.

In black and white sequence 16 the phone conversation is interrupted when Leonard removes a medical gauze dressing from his arm to reveal a tattoo which reads: 'Never answer the phone'. The narration shifts to a more communicative subjective mode and the audience hears the telephone dial tone as the unknown caller abruptly ends the call in response to Leonard asking 'Who is this?' The narration changes to an objective register with the final shot of the sequence, a wide shot of Leonard on the bed in the motel room. In the next colour scene Leonard is searching frantically for a pen. His search stops at the sound of a car door slamming and a subjective wide shot of Natalie arriving home. She explains that her bloody lip and nose are a consequence of visiting Dodd, the man looking for Jimmy, the money and the drugs. Leonard offers to warn Dodd off and tell him to look for a guy called Teddy. Natalie then tells Leonard that Dodd will probably be looking for him too as, under duress, she gave Dodd a description of Leonard's car. The narration highlights that Leonard has sore knuckles on one hand before he takes the description of Dodd from Natalie and leaves. The last four shots of the sequence repeat Leonard's attack on Teddy as he surprises him in the car. The next black and white sequence returns to Leonard and the insistent ringing of the phone, which he now refuses to answer. Natalie's manipulation of Leonard is presented in colour sequence 18. After hiding all the writing implements in the room and telling him that she is going to use him, Natalie goads Leonard into punching her face. The sore knuckles from the previous colour sequence are now explained. The spectator is forced to re-evaluate all the information from colour sequence 17 as it is now clear that Natalie's injuries were not inflicted by Dodd, but by Leonard, and that she has manipulated the situation for her own purposes. This scene also cues the audience to reconsider hypotheses about Teddy's role in the Dodd/Jimmy events. The scene ends with Leonard's frantic but fruitless search for a pen so that he can record what Natalie has done. The search is interrupted by the sound cue of the car door being closed and Natalie walking back to the house, so returning to the beginning of the previous colour sequence.

In black and white sequence 18 Bert informs Leonard that a policeman is trying to telephone him, but Leonard refuses to take any calls. In the colour sequence that follows, Leonard and Natalie arrive at Natalie's house. In a psychologically motivated flashback Leonard recounts the events of the night of the attack. Although the flashback repeats shots that have been used in previous scenes which recollect the incident, this version of events reveals a lot more communicativeness. Leonard's voiceover recounts the first few shots of the enacted events and the narration presents more information, including the crucial shots of a second man attacking Leonard from behind slamming him into the bathroom mirror. The flashback ends and Leonard tells to Natalie that the police did not believe that there was a second man. Having been presented with a psychologically motivated flashback which is presumed, on the basis of classical norms, to be reliable the audience is not channelled to hypothesise differently. Leonard photographs Natalie as she leaves the house then sits on a sofa watching television. A close-up of the tattoo 'Remember Sammy Jankis' is immediately followed by a shot of a hand tapping the air from a syringe and the torso of a woman in white out of focus in the background. Given the *syuzhet* presentation thus far, the audience is cued to hypothesise that the shot is a motivated flashback to Sammy preparing his wife's insulin injection. This shot is more ambiguous on a second viewing however, when the question of whether Leonard

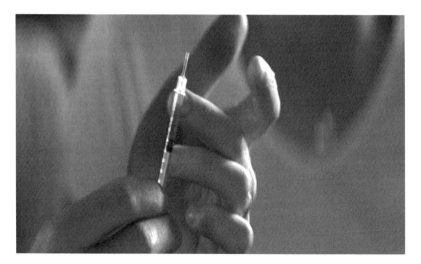

Figure 4 The audience is cued to hypothesise that the shot is a motivated flashback to Sammy Jankis preparing his wife's insulin injection but it is more ambiguous on a second viewing (© Newmarket / I Remember Productions)

administered insulin injections to his own wife has been foregrounded. The scene ends with a repeat shot of Natalie entering the house from the previous colour sequence. In the black and white sequence that follows, Leonard is agitated by the unanswered phone. An envelope slipped beneath his door has the words 'Take my call' on it and contains a photograph of Leonard smiling, his hands smeared with blood and pointing to the un-tattooed area of his chest over his heart.

In colour sequence 20, Natalie gives Leonard a tankard of beer, which he drinks. When prompted by her question, Leonard tells Natalie that the last thing he remembers is his wife dying. An extreme close-up of his wife's eye blinking beneath the plastic shower curtain precedes this. Natalie removes the tankard of beer on the pretext that it is dusty. In black and white sequence 20, Leonard answers the phone in a highly agitated state and again the narration suppresses information and does not give the spectator access to the caller's identity. Leonard's acknowledgement that the caller is a policeman is significant as the narration has drawn attention to an unidentified policeman through comments made by Leonard, Natalie and Bert in previous scenes. The scene ends after Leonard's desperate assertion, 'You don't believe someone with this condition' – a statement that has an enhanced narrational self-consciousness on a second viewing, cueing the spectator to consider the significance of claims to his own unreliability which Leonard makes throughout the film. In the next colour sequence Leonard arrives at a bar and is quizzed by Natalie about Jimmy and Teddy, both of whom Leonard denies all knowledge of, telling Natalie that he is unable to from new memories. Leonard sits at a table and looks at two Polaroids, but the narration remains objective whilst suppressing the information that Leonard is accessing at that point. Natalie tests Leonard, collecting spittle in a tankard of beer and serving it to him. Leonard drinks the beer and the scene ends with a repeated shot of Natalie removing the beer from the table from the previous colour sequence. Leonard returns to recounting the story of Sammy Jankis and his wife in black and white sequence 21. In the flashback Mrs Jankis attempts to prompt Sammy into remembering by repeatedly telling him that it is time for her insulin injection. Sammy administers the insulin three times, causing his wife to go into a coma. A shot of Sammy in a nursing home is accompanied by Leonard saying that Sammy doesn't know that his wife is dead and his own admission that he had been wrong about the couple. Leonard explains to the unknown caller that to cope with the condition Sammy and he both 'fake' recognition if they feel that they are supposed to know someone, in order to seem less of 'a freak'. At this point Leonard is briefly substituted for Sammy sitting in the nursing home.

In the next colour scene Leonard arrives at a tattoo parlour to have 'Fact 6' done, the voiceover repeating the licence plate number, 'SG137IU'. Teddy arrives and tells Leonard that he needs to leave town because a 'bad cop' is looking for him. Teddy claims that this police officer has been calling Leonard, put the Polaroid photograph under his door and has been manipulating him by suggesting that Jimmy Grantz is the drug dealer that Leonard is looking for. Teddy says that he is a police informer and this is how he has access to the information. He gives Leonard a bag of clothes and tells him to leave town, but after looking at his Polaroid of Teddy and the note 'Don't believe his lies', Leonard decides to ignore his advice. Finding a beermat with the message 'Come by later, Natalie' in the pocket of his jacket, he heads for Ferdy's bar. There, Natalie approaches Leonard's car and initially mistakes Lenny for Jimmy. The scene closes with repeated shots from the beginning of the previous colour sequence of Leonard in the car and Natalie putting rubbish in a dumpster.

Black and white sequence 22 begins by channelling the audience to re-evaluate Teddy's claims in the tattoo parlour about the bad cop's manipulation of Leonard. Talking to a police officer on the phone, Leonard recounts what he is being told, that Jimmy deals in drugs from the bar where his girlfriend works. This information now fits with Teddy's earlier claims that Leonard is being set up. Leonard agrees to meet the police officer in the motel lobby, packs his belongings and walks to the front desk to find Teddy waiting for him. Teddy claims that he is in fact Officer Gammell and the two walk to the car. Leonard takes a picture of Teddy, the Polaroid that has been one of the crucial visual signposts throughout the film. He writes 'Teddy' on the front of the Polaroid and a phone number Teddy gives him with details of the rendezvous where Jimmy is going to be.

Leonard drives to the deserted building, gets out of his station wagon and enters the building. A car pulls up outside and as Leonard goes to see who it is, the narration cuts to a shot of Leonard's wife in colour, echoing Leonard's movements and going to look out of a window. The status of this shot is unclear as it is in colour and therefore belongs to a flashback from within the colour plot-line (as all flashbacks in the black and white sequences have also been in black and white). The narration cuts back to a subjective shot of the Jaguar that Leonard has been driving in the colour sequences, pulling up outside the building. A man gets out of the car calling for 'Teddy'. A shot of Leonard looking away from the window in thought is intercut with another colour shot of his wife sitting down and making a similar head movement. A third colour shot of his wife echoes the black and white shot of Leonard from the rear as he walks to meet Jimmy. Referring to Leonard as 'memory man' Jimmy recognises him and asks him where Teddy is. Leonard forces Jimmy to remove his clothes and Jimmy, now concerned, says that he has $200,000 in the car. Leonard refuses the money and when Jimmy asks what he does want, a fourth colour shot of Leonard's wife at a table and turning round to address someone accompanies Leonard's assertion that he wants his life back. Leonard throttles Jimmy and a colour flashback of Leonard's wife being attacked is included in the sequence. In his attempts to stop Leonard Jimmy scratches his face but Leonard prevails and when Jimmy stops moving, Leonard photographs his body and puts on Jimmy's shirt. As the Polaroid develops the scene changes from black and white to colour, marking the point where the two plot-lines, and therefore time-lines, meet. Leonard dresses in the rest of Jimmy's clothes and dumps the body in the basement of the building. As he drags him downstairs, Leonard thinks he hears Jimmy say 'Sammy'. Teddy arrives at the deserted building and Leonard is now uncertain about what he has done. Telling Teddy that someone in the basement is hurt Leonard asks, 'Do I know you?' to which Teddy replies no and shows him his police badge, saying that he is a cop. Teddy checks Jimmy's body and declares that he is dead, but this is not confirmed by Leonard and the narration does not give any cues to confirm that Jimmy is dead at this point. Instead the focus turns to Leonard's realisation that Teddy lied to him when he said that he didn't know him and Leonard hits him across the head with the camera. Teddy then admits that he is a cop and that he found and lured Jimmy Grantz to the abandoned building for Leonard, but Leonard disputes Teddy's claim that Jimmy is in fact John G. Teddy proceeds to offer a version of events that forces the spectator to reconsider most of their hypotheses up to this point. In Teddy's account Leonard's wife survives the incident, an assertion that is accompanied by the close-up shot of her eye blinking beneath the plastic shower curtain, a shot that has previously been attributed to Leonard's memory of her dying. In Teddy's version of events he asserts that it was Leonard's wife who had diabetes and did not believe his condition, not Mrs Jankis. Flashback shots present Leonard preparing an insulin injection, and his wife after the attack pulling away the shower curtain and still alive lying on the bathroom floor. In one version of his remembered events Leonard injects the top of his wife's thigh, in a second recollection he revises the memory and pinches the top of her thigh instead, repeating his memory from the night beside the fire. Teddy claims that Leonard remembers only what he wants to be true and that he has altered his recollections through repetition and conditioning. When Leonard states 'My wife wasn't diabetic', Teddy response is 'Are you sure?' Teddy then reveals that he and Leonard killed the real John G. a year earlier but Leonard did not remember. Leonard looks at the Polaroid of himself pointing at the untattooed area of his chest, an image that Teddy claims to have taken when they killed the real John G. Teddy then asserts that Leonard has removed pages from the police file to create a puzzle that he cannot solve and makes the point that there are many John G.'s for Leonard to kill and that even he, Teddy, is a John G. – John Edward Gammell.

Outside the derelict building the spectator is given access to Leonard's thoughts. In his interior monologue Leonard claims that he is not a killer and asks whether he can let himself forget about the killing of Jimmy Grantz or what Teddy has told him. After emptying the bullets from his gun onto the car seat, Leonard writes 'Don't believe his lies' on the reverse of Teddy's picture. He then burns the photo of Jimmy's corpse and decides that Teddy will be the next John G. he will hunt. To these ends he writes another note to get a tattoo of Teddy's car licence plate number – his 6 Fact. Despite Teddy's remonstrations, Leonard then photographs the Jaguar car, puts the gun on top of a box of money in the boot of the car and drives away. As he drives, Leonard's voiceover asserts that he has to believe that his actions still have meaning. This is accompanied by four shots of Leonard, his wife lying on him and caressing a tattoo over his heart which reads 'I've done it'. Seeing a tattoo parlour, Leonard pulls up outside and looks at the Fact 6 tattoo reminder note.

Ambiguity, independence and multiple viewings

In various ways *Memento* conforms to certain norms of classical narrative having two distinct plot-lines which converge towards the end of the film, a three-act structure, a goal-oriented protagonist, a high level of redundancy, causally-linked scenes and a chain of events. Where *Memento* deviates from classical norms is in its temporal reordering, episodic structure, effect–cause relationships, strict adherence to subjective narration, and the resultant privilege given to ambiguity over certainty. Whilst the two plot-lines are distinct, one being in colour and the other in black and white, the reverse colour plot-line hampers easy comprehension of the film. The viewer is forced to mentally reorder a series of events which are being shown in reverse, a process that makes apparent the centrality of memory in narrative comprehension. Because the flow of events is made especially difficult to comprehend the audience is put in the protagonist's position, struggling to hold all the information in mind and piece together fragments to form a coherent story.

In colour sequence 13 a dissolve to early morning suggests that Leonard has sat by the fire all the night and this point in the narration presents the passage of time in a mode that conforms to classical norms of ellipsis. Elsewhere, however, duration in *Memento* is unclear because the reversed episodic structure of the colour sequences also alternates with black and white sequences which come earlier in the chronology. Consequently, the shifts from day to night, dusk to dawn are disorienting because the narration does not present events in a linear trajectory that passes through the various parts of the day in order, scene by scene.[46] In short, the *syuzhet* makes the fabula duration confusing because the episodic structure challenges easy comprehension of story time. This approximates Leonard's experience of time, and both he and Teddy remark on occasions that Leonard has no real concept of how much time has elapsed since the night of the attack.

The final sequence of the film forces a major re-evaluation of the narrative information and opens up possible hypotheses about Leonard and his actions. However, the film's ambiguity is not solely a consequence of Teddy's final revelatory dialogue which forces spectators to revise their hypotheses. Instead the ambiguities in *Memento* are produced by the subversion of narrational norms as well as the establishment of particular intrinsic norms such as the *syuzhet* presentation of external flashbacks in both plot-lines. It is these manipulations of the fabula that bear further consideration because they are central to the ambiguities of *Memento*, Flashbacks are a narrative convention attributable to character subjectivity and usually psychologically motivated as a memory or recollection. In *Memento* flashbacks are a narrational strategy primarily used to tell the Sammy Jankis story and to give the spectator access to Leonard's memories of his wife and the events that occurred on the night of the attack, all of which are external flashbacks that depict events that have occurred prior to the first event (Leonard in the anonymous motel room) presented by the *syuzhet*. In broad terms, psychologically motivated flashbacks within classical narrative tend to be reliable and attributable to character recollection. Edward Branigan, however, draws attention to the various levels of objectivity and subjectivity that complicate the flashback and highlights the complex relationships between flashback and voice-over. For instance, flashbacks may be objective summaries of a voiceover, or the character reliving an experience, they may be equivalent to the fears and desires of the character's unconscious, or a mixture of objective and subjective images of events.[47] When Teddy gives an alternative account of Leonard's past at the end of the film, the objectivity and subjectivity of the flashbacks are unsettled and the flashbacks acquire even more indeterminacy. The Sammy Jankis story, which has been told in flashbacks that re-enact the events recounted by the voiceover, is therefore rendered ambiguous.

Leonard exists in the same diegetic space as Sammy in a number of the scenes where he watches Sammy administer the insulin injections and undertake testing whilst the voiceover recounts the enacted events. As such the flashbacks initially may be determined as an objective summary. From Teddy's account, however, the status of the flashbacks alters and the final exposition revises them as potentially subjective and the product of Leonard's unconscious or imagination. Assessing the contradictions of the Sammy Jankis flashbacks on a second viewing the spectator may then be cued to attach greater significance to the flashback of Sammy in hospital where Leonard briefly substitutes for Sammy. This shot is open to possible hypotheses that support either the objective or subjective status of the Sammy Jankis story: either Leonard has substituted Sammy for himself in his account of events and his repressed unconscious reveals the substitution, or the Sammy/Leonard switch is an artistically motivated choice to express a common experience between two people with the same condition. The shots of Leonard and his wife at the end of the film are similarly open to question. Are they a flashforward and Leonard's wife is actually alive, or are they the fantasies of Leonard the killer? In this sense, ambiguity is derived from the overlapping and shifting objective/subjective status of flashbacks and from a lack of cues to enable the spectator to resolve the contradictions between what is seen in the flashbacks and what is heard in the dialogue.

In addition, the Sammy Jankis flashbacks are equivocal by the end of the film because the narration has expended so much effort to establish Teddy as unreliable, ensuring that the audience identifies with Leonard. To these ends the spectator has witnessed Leonard being manipulated by each of the characters Teddy, Bert and Natalie whilst the subjective shots, restricted narration, strategic access to Leonard's thoughts and extensive use of voiceover have channelled the spectator to identify with him. The primacy effect and Leonard's establishment early in the film as the primary agent of knowledge cue the audience to accept the veracity of his account in both dialogue and flashback to the extent that even when the narration explicitly shows Leonard deceiving himself and setting himself up to kill Teddy, his account of events prior to the incident retains plausibility. The investment that the spectator makes in Leonard is, in large part, dependent on such classical norms and it is therefore both adherence to and subversion of these that are exploited to produce ambiguity.

Nowhere is the film's ambivalence more apparent than in the revision of Leonard's memories and especially his recollection of pinching/injecting his wife's thigh. The audience is presented with two contradictory versions of an event, a narrational device that leaves the film open-ended and asks the spectator to decide which account is true. However, absolute construction of the fabula is inhibited by the *syuzhet* as the *syuzhet*'s presentation of events make possible two (or more) fabulas. Ambiguity resides in the narrational gap between Leonard's life prior to the incident and finding himself in an anonymous motel room. Everything presented between those two points is open to question. By way of contrast, the causal chain that follows events from Leonard in the anonymous motel room to his killing of Teddy is, although difficult to comprehend due to the reverse ordering, robust. Watching the film a second time the spectator is not required to assimilate the information about Leonard's condition and is cued to follow the causal chain, having a different schema with which to create and test hypothesis from that which was available on first viewing. On a second viewing, therefore, the audience is cued to begin looking for answers to new questions of who Leonard is and what he has done to the extent that the narrative resistance to absolute truth gives rise to the questions that inform subsequent film viewings.

Memento's reflexivity alerts us to the conditions of cinematic viewing by negotiating and resisting classical norms and refusing to adhere to a clear delineation between objective and subjective narration giving rise to multiple and indeterminate fabula. For some scholars and critics *Memento* is a hybrid narrative form. J. J. Murphy (2007) pursues this line, suggesting that independent feature films have developed distinct modes of storytelling that challenge conventions such as the three-act paradigm, causal relationships and linear progression.[48] He proposes that independent cinema has a particular 'narrational strategy' that is not a 'unique and separate category, but instead represents a hybrid form that bridges the divide between classical Hollywood and art cinema by freely incorporating elements from both of them'.[49] In this sense, narrative complexity is established as a key aspect of the alternative vision and aesthetic offered by independent cinema since the 1990s.

Whilst it is true to say that narrative complexity can be closely associated with independent filmmaking, in light of the wider trend towards complex narratives across a range of screen-based entertainment, including commercial studio films such as *The Matrix*, it is difficult to sustain an argument that such films represent a distinct narrational strategy attributable predominantly to independent cinema. Moreover, even though many films which sport alternative narrative structures may indeed come from the independent sector, these do not represent the majority of independent films and it may be pertinent to resist the temptation to extrapolate too widely from critical or box office successes alone. That said, what *Memento* makes apparent is that the independent sector is better positioned to take risks with complex narratives, a point that David Hesmondhalgh implies when he argues that 'smaller firms are potentially more dynamic and able to innovate than the large conglomerates'.[50] It is also the case that *Memento* was strategically important in terms of demonstrating to distributors and the majors that a complex narrative could achieve mainstream success at the US box office. Furthermore, the later addition of Teddy's revelatory dialogue at the end of the film, which for many offered a potential resolution to *Memento*'s ambiguity, was supported by the film's producers, who were hired specifically to ensure that the film did not veer too far towards the art film end of the indie spectrum. In this regard, *Memento*'s 'narrational strategy' cannot be detached from the prescribed indie/commercial context within which it was developed.

David Bordwell (2006) and Kristin Thompson (1999) reject the notion that complex narratives signal a departure from existing narrative techniques and both seek to recover such films within the bounds of classical narrative. Bordwell argues 'most of the daring storytelling we find in modern American film offers legible variations on well-entrenched strategies for presenting time, space, goal achievement, causal connection, and the like. Nothing comes from nothing',[51] and commenting on the recurring influences between art cinema and Hollywood Bordwell argues that 'art-cinema devices have been selectively applied to films which remain firmly grounded in classical genres'.[52] *Memento* borrows from art cinema narration in various ways yet remains firmly anchored to mainstream conventions such that ambiguity and complexity are crucial elements of spectator pleasure whilst classical norms maintain spectator familiarity. The innovative reversed structure is disorienting yet works to sustain Leonard as a goal-oriented protagonist with a realistic motivation for hunting John G., creating causal lines, curiosity and suspense. Flashbacks, dreams, memories, recollections and the restricted narration negotiate a space between classical and alternative conventions that produces ambiguity.

Crucially, the conditions of film viewing are now such that ambiguity can be more easily accommodated by commercial cinema. Elsaesser expands the geographical and industrial specificity of complex storytelling beyond what he describes as 'a Europe–East Asia–American independents triangle' to suggest that such films transcend genre, *auteur* and national cinema and are evident in mainstream and independent cinema as well as (HBO-financed) television to point towards a new form of spectator address that challenges 'classical spectator positions . . . and their related cinematic regimes or techniques'.[53] Elsaesser's argument fits well with assertions made by Christopher Nolan in an interview in 2001 when he commented that he was acutely aware of the ways in which new technologies were shaping film art. Heavily influenced by the introduction of VHS when he was growing up, Nolan pointed out: 'We're the last generation who remembers a time when you couldn't record television, you couldn't control time like that. We remember the shift.' And commenting on DVD he noted that 'A director of my generation is much freer to jump around and give people information in short bursts . . . So it should have layers, it should have cinematic density that rewards multiple viewings.'[54] Nolan's comments demonstrate filmmakers' awareness of the changing conditions of film viewing and the potential for narrative experimentation made possible by technological developments. *Memento* was always intended to be a 'DVD-enabled' film that, like other complex narratives, attended to the changing conditions of film spectatorship and the trend towards multiple viewings. This allowed for the appropriation of art cinema devices which fragment the unity of the film discourse, creating dissonance between what is seen and what is heard in such a way that *Memento* pushes against but does not exceed the norms of classical narrative.

4 *Memento* as *Noir*

Memento's exploration of memory and identity would seem to align it with a rash of contemporaneous texts, including *Eternal Sunshine of the Spotless Mind* (Gondry, 2004), *Being John Malkovitch* (Jonze, 1999), *The Machinist* (Anderson, 2004), *A Beautiful Mind* (Howard, 2001) and *The Butterfly Effect* (Bress and Gruber, 2004), as well as with earlier films such as *Angel Heart* (Parker, 1987), *Total Recall* (Verhoeven, 1990) and *Last Year at Marienbad* ([*L année dernière à Marienbad*] Resnais, 1961). However, *Memento*'s narrative structure, flashbacks, voiceover, dream sequences and the generic tropes of the detective thriller, coupled with an unreliable narrator, morally ambiguous hero, *femme fatale* and corrupt cop, all nod selfconsciously towards *film noir*. Marketing materials referred to the film as *noir*, whilst in interviews Christopher Nolan spoke of being a fan of the 'classic *noir*' *Double Indemnity* (Wilder, 1944), and production notes for the film described *Memento* as '*film noir* pared down to its most visceral elements, setting its hero adrift in a sea of confusion and paranoia that bit-by-bit causes the audience to question everything that happens right before their eyes'.[1] In critical reviews the film was variously described as a 'puzzle movie', an 'amnesia thriller', a 'noirish thriller,' '*noir*', 'meta-*noir*', 'neo-*noir*', '*nouveau noir*' and a 'revenge thriller' that 'uses a favourite plot device of postwar Fruedian *film noir*'.[2] The reviews illustrated a dizzying array of category descriptors, which in turn highlight the problematic classification of films within generic boundaries and as *noir*.

In his examination of *film noir*, Steve Neale argues that 'as a single phenomenon, *noir*, in my view, never existed'.[3] He goes on to explain that the various features that have been associated with noir are so widely dispersed across a range of trends, genres and cycles that they render imprecise 'the contours of the larger *noir* canon'.[4] Neale does, however, propose that whilst *noir* is not a genre, 'the phenomenon of neo-*noir* – itself a vehicle for this fantasy – is much more real, not only as a phenomenon but also as a genre'.[5] This chapter situates *Memento* as neo-*noir* to examine the ways in which the film 'relate[s] to or draw[s] upon the notion, the image and the putative conventions of *film noir*, and directly or indirectly, on some of the films featured centrally within most versions of the basic noir canon'[6] in order to reflect on the extent to which *Memento* may offer a commentary on contemporary identity bounded by discourses of gender and disability.

Noir and Neo-*noir*

In an interview about *Memento* Christopher Nolan commented:

> To many people, *film noir* has become this nostalgic image of guys in rain coats and fedoras coming down alleyways. But when you go back and look at the films, you realise they were very contemporary stories, imbued with exaggerated everyday fears. I wanted to do a modern *noir* which would reawaken some of that paranoia in a slightly different way.[7]

Nolan's historicising of *film noir* as an expression of the anxieties of a society at a specific moment in time suggests that it is both mobile and elastic enough to accommodate meaningful appropriations within different contexts. Nolan's claim seems to run counter to Fredric Jameson's argument that the contemporary mobilisation of past styles is a form of intertextual referencing which functions as nostalgia for a past that was in itself a fiction. The 'random cannibalization of all the styles of the past', according to Jameson, produces a depthless pastiche which reflects the inability of a culture to produce new styles or deal with current experience.[8] As such the 'nostalgia mode' effaces the present in favour of a simulation of 'pastness'. James Naremore proposes that Jameson's account of the postmodern appropriation of style as the cultural expression of late capitalism seems too pessimistic. Whilst he concedes that there are a number of contemporary films that borrow stylistic references from *film noir* in much the way that Jameson suggests, Naremore argues that 'the past has different constituencies and different uses, and we need to consider retro films on an individual basis'.[9] To these ends, he contends that *film noir* appears in many guises and is bounded by various genres and forms of critical classification such as melodrama and crime drama, and as such *noir* is characterised by its flexibility of appropriation. He suggests that '*film noir* occupies a liminal space somewhere between Europe and America, between high modernism and "blood melodrama", and between low-budget crime movies and art cinema'.[10] In this sense, rather than grouping films together as *noir* and expecting all of them to adopt certain generic norms, individual films will accommodate aspects of *noir* in multiple ways, including ahistorical postmodern pastiche alongside other historicised forms.

Elsewhere, *noir* is proposed as a sensibility within films that inflects a general, historically situated set of anxieties about the presence of a gendered, racial or sexual 'other', configured as dangerous in the white middle-class experience of the city and its margins. The concerns of classic *films noirs* with women's social power were expressed and resolved through the *femme fatale*, whilst anxieties about racial and sexual otherness were implicitly invoked primarily through their absence. Writing about the dominance of a white male culture within the structure of Hollywood film, E. Ann Kaplan suggests that 'While the specificity of fears of women, homosexuals and people of colour are different, all three share a similarity as marginalised by the white centre'.[11] Mike Chopra-Gant warns that arguments about the collective expression of nationwide anxieties can be problematic if too enthusiastically embraced within accounts of *noir*. Regarding the postwar era specifically, he suggests that 'While *film noir* may register the anxieties of Americans . . . it is considerably over-simplifying the matter to conclude that the anxiety undoubtedly evident in numerous *films noirs* was Hollywood's – and indeed, American society's – only response to this situation'.[12] Anxiety was not, he concludes, the overriding sensibility expressed by American films during what is considered to be the classic *noir* era, but Chopra-Gant agrees with others that cynicism and bleakness did pervade the *films noirs* of the time. Foster Hirsch argues that paranoia has remained the defining feature of *noir* and proposes that, 'It is in this sense that *noir* has continued to thrive: *noir* names a knot of feelings and intuition – dread, uncertainty, paranoia – that won't go away. And postmodern life has cooperated by continuing to fuel numerous anxieties easily subsumed under *noir*.'[13] However, the paranoias of the late twentieth and early twenty-first centuries differ substantially from those of the immediate postwar era. In order to address these significant, differences, whilst recognising a continued incorporation of *noir*, Hirsch and others propose a distinction between classic *noir* and neo-*noir*.

The classic *noir* era is considered to span the early 1940s to the late 1950s, ending in 1958 with Orson Welles' *Touch of Evil*. Mark T. Conard suggests that the term 'neo-*noir*' should be used to describe any post-1958 film with *noir* themes and sensibility, although he acknowledges that this encompasses a huge corpus.[14] This potentially vast number of films notwithstanding, there is general agreement between advocates of neo-*noir* that a '*noir* sensibility' is both recognisable and present in films made after the classic era. Characterised by chiaroscuro lighting and tilted camera angles, *noir* referenced the visual style of German Expressionism from within the middle-class experience of American towns and cities. Here the mundane became menacing as sunlight was sliced through venetian blinds, streets and alleys were made dangerously slick with rain, suburban life was constrained and suffocating, and when night eventually gave way to the occasional summer day it was ominously stifling, harsh and unforgiving. The stylised images conveyed disordered moral values, paranoia, bleakness, cynicism and pessimistic introspection and were populated by a host of distinct characters: *femmes fatales*, disillusioned anti-heroes, jealous husbands and corrupt cops. Governed by the Production Code, *noir* was occupied with morally ambiguous characters who were inevitably punished at the end of the film. Sexually provocative women who lured men into criminal activity, often murder, would predictably die showing no remorse for their actions, whilst the anti-hero would often realise his moral failings in the final scenes, thereby escaping death.

Hirsch argues that neo-*noir* has remained permeated with the paranoia, characters and stylised imagery of *noir* but now that the Production Code no longer exits, is free to allow morally flawed characters to succeed.[15] The *femme fatale* can enjoy her manipulation and get away with it; crimes, even murder, can go unpunished and the criminals can prosper under a different moral regime from that which had governed classic *noir*. Neo-*noir* does, however, have more self-consciousness than *film noir*, which was a retrospectively applied label.[16] Contemporary filmmakers, unlike those of the classic era, know what *noir* 'is' and for this reason neo-*noir* is able to appropriate references in the way that Jameson describes – as stylistic plunderings of the past. Not limited to black and white photography neo-*noir* also makes use of stylised colour, rejects technological display but utilises the pace of contemporary editing patterns as well as more mobile camerawork in comparison to its classic *noir* predecessors, and so 'Noir still provides a low-budget showcase for novice filmmakers'.[17]

Neo-*noir* and gender

The description of neo-*noir* fits *Memento* with glove-like ease: Leonard, the ex-insurance investigator turned amateur detective apparently in pursuit of his wife's killer selfconsciously references classic *film noir's* predilection for the private eye and anti-hero. Teddy, the corrupt cop, is another *noir* archetype, as is Natalie, the *femme fatale*, whilst Catherine Shelby, Leonard's wife, is the opposing female character. Janey Place's description of the 'woman as redeemer' in *noir* maps particularly well on the character of Catherine in *Memento.* Place writes that such a character is

generally visually passive and static. Often, in order to offer this alternative to the nightmare landscape of *film noir,* she herself must not be part of it. She is then linked to the pastoral environment of open spaces, light, and safely characterized by even, flat, high-key lighting. Often this is an idealized dream of the past and she exists only in memory, but sometimes this idealization exists as a real alternative.[18]

In *Memento* Catherine exists in Leonard's memory, detached from the realities of his daily experience yet constrained by the controlled construction of his recollections, a point that is highlighted at the end of the film when Teddy challenges Leonard's memories. During a scene in the diner when Natalie meets Leonard to give him information about John G., memories of Catherine are distinguished in Leonard's flashback by being imbued with warmer tones which contrast with the colder blues of his daily existence. Loose framing and hand-held camerawork place Catherine in a domestic kitchen setting during these recollections. Sunlight catches her face and as she looks through a window her face is obscured by the reflected images of the trees and greenery outside. Leonard's recollections of his wife take two distinct forms: the images of the passive, idealised woman in a garden, a kitchen and a bedroom, and those of her on the night of the attack, where she is tightly framed between shots of a white tiled floor, her face fragmented into close-ups of a mouth gasping and an eye blinking. Colour shots of Catherine also contrast with the black and white photography of a later scene when Leonard meets Jimmy Grantz at the deserted building. These shots of Catherine disrupt the scene as colour punctuations from Leonard's memory which continue to present his wife as recalled fragments which Leonard describes to Natalie when he tells her in the dinner, during the flashback, 'You can just feel the details. The bits and pieces you never bothered to put into words. And you can feel these extreme moments, even if you don't want to. You put these together and you get the feel of a person.' Catherine is, in Leonard's memory, always 'bits and pieces', partially constructed and denied full realisation within the narrative.

Leonard and Catherine's idealised relationship is potentially unstable
though and in a flashback when he questions why Catherine wants to
re-read a book, she responds: 'Don't be a prick. I'm not reading it to
annoy you. I enjoy it.' There is enough in this short exchange to suggest
that the marriage is not as perfect as Leonard desires it to be and *Memento*
updates the *noir* archetype of the 'good woman' with a slightly more
problematic reading of contemporary marital relations. Nonetheless,
Leonard is reunited with Catherine at the end of the film in three highly
ambiguous shots, where the couple lie on a bed, Catherine's head resting
on Leonard's chest as she caresses the tattoo across his heart which reads
'I've done it', signifying retribution and Leonard's redemption. As Place
writes about the 'woman as redeemer': 'She offers the possibility of inte-
gration for the alienated, lost man into the stable world of secure values,
roles and identities.'[19]

Whereas Catherine signifies stability and domesticity, Natalie is the
controlling *femme fatale* – independent, manipulative and dangerous.
Cool, aloof and strong, it is Natalie's manipulation of Leonard that is
grist for the *noir* mill. When Leonard arrives at her house demanding
to know who Dodd is, the events are managed by Natalie, who eventually calms Leonard and the scene turns from confrontation to intimacy
between the two. Natalie controls the situation, taking Leonard over to
the mirror, removing his shirt to read his tattoos, whilst close-ups follow
her fingers as she traces them across his bare chest, all the while looking
at their reflection. The mirrored reflection of the *femme fatale* in *films
noirs* acts as a metaphor for duplicity or narcissism, about which Place
comments:

> They are visually split, thus not to be trusted. Further, this motif contrib-
> utes to the murky confusion of *film noir*: nothing and no one is what it seems.
> Compositions in which reflections are stronger than the actual woman . . . help
> to create the mood of threat and fear.[20]

Both Leonard and Natalie are reflected in the mirror, although Natalie
is clearly in control of the composition of the reflection, placing Leonard
in position then moving in front of him then behind him. Faced with his
own reflection Leonard is still, immobile, in contrast to Natalie's fluid
seduction as she walks around him, undressing and caressing him. As
such, the power relations between the two are expressed through the
passive and active roles that each adopts. In the preceding scene (and
therefore the morning following Natalie's seduction) Leonard wakes to

find himself in bed with her. The first thing he sees is a bird in a cage, a familiar *noir* motif which points towards Leonard's impending entrapment. Natalie gets out of the bed and sits in front of a mirror where her reflection is privileged for the remainder of the scene. All physical contact between Leonard and Natalie is instigated and controlled by her both in the bed and out of it, and when Natalie eventually turns from the mirror to give Leonard a note she pulls him towards her to kiss him and tells him that, despite his assertions to the contrary, he will remember her.

Of all the Polaroid pictures that Leonard carries, the one of Natalie stands apart. Leonard takes the picture from across a room as Natalie leaves the house. In the image her face is consequently partly obscured by shadow, a signifier of her character as the morally ambivalent *femme fatale*. Natalie is captured in the picture, and therefore as Leonard's prosthetic memory, in such a way as to offer a symbolic opposition with his recollections of Catherine, who appears in bright natural light. The dark/light symbolism continues to be mapped onto the women's bodies, with Natalie dressed in dark colours whilst Catherine wears lighter clothes and sensible, asexual white underwear. By way of comparison, in later scenes Natalie's black bra is visible beneath a sheer black, cropped top, referencing the visual iconography of the sexual power of the *femme fatale* deployed in classic *film noir*. Natalie's manipulation of Leonard does not, however, work through seduction; instead, it is through sexualised violence when she provokes Leonard into punching her, an act which maintains allusions to masochism which is inflected throughout the film. When Leonard refuses to kill Dodd, Natalie tells him that she is going to use him and will enjoy doing it, a caution that is redolent with sexual overtones. As Natalie walks round Leonard who, as in the scene in front of the mirror, once again stands unmoving she taunts him, suggesting that his short-term memory loss is a consequence of venereal disease which he has acquired from his wife. Natalie insinuates that Catherine was promiscuous and calls her a whore, telling Leonard that he is 'a freak' and 'a retard', unable to stop the manipulation which is now inevitable. Natalie says, 'I can say whatever the fuck I want. You won't remember. We can still be best friends, maybe even lovers', at which point Leonard punches her, a blow which knocks her to the floor.

In *film noir*, the *femme fatale* suffers for her manipulations; in neo-*noir* she gets away with it. Hitting Natalie places Leonard squarely in the morally compromised shoes of the *noir* anti-hero cajoled into abusive behaviour by the duplicitous *femme fatale*. Yet, the notion that Natalie 'deserves' the physical abuse is problematised by her enjoyment of it. She does not suffer at Leonard's hands but derives satisfaction from being able to manipulate the situation and generate the violent response she seeks. In this sense, an excess of masochistic desire is implied by Natalie continuing to goad Leonard even after he has grabbed her face and caused her lip to bleed. Whilst Natalie may express masochistic desire, in a reference to *noir*'s displacement of sexual frustration onto violent action, Leonard's inability to do anything other than punch Natalie alludes to the impotence of the *noir* anti-hero. The narration implies exactly this when Leonard gets out of the bed that he has shared with Natalie and is wearing his trousers. Although Natalie reminds him that he has a registration number tattooed at the top of his thigh, and so she must have seen him undressed, the implication that they have not had sex remains.

Leonard's relationships with women are complex. During act 2 of the film, Leonard hires an escort and re-enacts the events of the night of his wife's rape. This ambivalent scene is given some context by Leonard who, in an interior monologue in another scene, says that he can't 'remember to forget', suggesting that the re-enactment functions as a form of trauma therapy. However the re-staging of the night of the rape is entirely contrived and controlled by Leonard and enabled by his indiscriminate purchase of an escort, thereby, blurring the line between therapy and sexual fantasy. The ease with which he hires the escort and directs her actions indicates that this is something Leonard has done on other occasions and the re-enactment of the attack is thus problematised as a rape fantasy. Leonard wakes when the bathroom door slams, sees his wife's clock, book and teddy bear and calls to her. He appears to remember a detail from the night of the attack, his wife being suffocated and struggling under the plastic shower curtain. Yet Leonard could not have witnessed this moment himself as he was not in the bathroom during the attack and thus the image of his wife may be construed as imagined. Leonard walks to the bathroom and listens at the door, his question 'OK in there?' suggesting that he is imagining the sounds that he heard on the night of the attack, those of his wife being assaulted. He opens the door to see the escort snorting cocaine whilst sitting on the toilet. Re-invoking Leonard's barely sublimated fantasy she asks, 'Was it good for you?'

In his imagining of the night of the attack, Leonard hears what occurs but does not witness the rape, one of many incidents in *Memento* where there is a discrepancy between what is seen and what is heard. These ruptures give rise to ambiguity and indeterminacy so that Leonard's fantasy is always incomplete and unfulfilled. By way of contrast, the rape itself is the only sexual act that is consistently referred to unambiguously throughout the film; in flashback, in dialogue and as a tattoo on Leonard's body which reads 'John G raped and murdered my wife'. The tattoo across his chest is in reverse and can only be read when Leonard contemplates his reflection in a mirror. As with the *femme fatale*, mirrors and reflections symbolically refer to notions of identity in *noir*. Leonard's identity is fragmented so that one aspect of his sense of self is always intrinsically bound up with the rape and his reflected self is coextensive with sexual violence. Nonetheless, each of Leonard's relationships with women suggests sexual impotence, a motif that is further reinforced by his memory condition, which renders Leonard socially incapacitated.

One reading that *Memento* makes possible is the suggestion that memory loss is a form of symbolic impotence which functions to offer a commentary on contemporary masculinity. In this sense, Leonard's identity is effaced by his impairment, which draws on constructions of hegemonic masculinity, idealised as strong and able, whilst disablement suggests sexual abjection of the impaired 'other' and a corruption of the social norms of 'maleness' – a discursive constellation that draws attention to the intersection of gender and disability within constructions of identity. Hegemonic masculinity is exclusionary and shaped by what it disallows, legitimating the subordination of sexual, racial, gendered or impaired otherness to an idealised version of masculinity which, thematically at least, aligns with certain readings of the ideological expression of masculinity in classic *noir* narratives. Leonard's impairment is cognitive rather than physical. Thus *Memento* eludes one popular trope of disabled masculinity found in films other than *noir* – the physical impairment used in Hitchcock's *Rear Window* (1954) for instance – in favour of another which has been favoured by *film noir*, that of the amnesiac. During the 1940s films such as *Spellbound* (Hitchcock, 1945), *Black Angel* (Neill, 1946) *Somewhere in the Night* (Mankiewicz, 1946) and *The Crooked Way* (Florey, 1949) all utilised the theme of amnesia, and whilst these films expressed anxieties about masculinity, they were also set within a particular social context. The topic of amnesia framed by wartime and postwar discourses had a specific historically-situated resonance and set of meanings.[21] This suggests that particular discourses of masculinity are at work within different historical contexts and the amnesiac hero has a separate symbolic currency within neo-*noir* which it did not have in *noir* of the classic era. As such, the notion of a fixed, unchanging, idealised masculinity is contested by the various histories that attend to the array of discourses that construct multiple masculinities. From this plurality of discourses, the 'New Man' and the 'Retributive Man' emerged in the last decades of the twentieth century and these discourses provide a way of thinking about memory and identity in *Memento*.

The discourse of the New Man arose from the visual recoding of masculinity which took place within advertising during the 1990s and which was part of the commodification of men's lifestyle practices, particularly those associated with male grooming. New Man imagery permeated popular culture and intersected with a growing men's anti-sexist movement which had emerged in the 1970s, giving rise to a reconfiguration of sexuality in relation to fatherhood and care-giving.[22] The discourse expressed less oppressive relations of power with women and other men, although race and impairment remained the absent 'other' within New Man imagery. The New Man contrasted with earlier constructions of masculinity such as those epitomised by the *Rambo* films and the concept of the Retributive Man. This construction offered an idealised version of masculinity that espoused emotional attachments in favour of an individual assertion of power, often expressed through violent action that was configured as heroic and coupled with imagery of the excessively masculine body which was muscular and strong and able to withstand sometimes self-inflicted physical pain. With a plurality of available masculinities in play, Toerien and Durrheim argue that:

Masculinity is no longer seen as a fixed way of being, but as a field of conflict that men have to traverse in a quest for coherence. The conflicting representations of masculinity in the 'new man' and 'retributive man' discourses do not denote different types of men or personalities (Connell, 1995), but rather different cultural resources that individual men draw on in their everyday lives. The discourses provide a range of subject positions for men to take up, and enacting masculinity in any particular context thus involves figuring out what it means to be a man.[23]

It is this 'quest for coherence' through a plurality of identities that Leonard pursues within *Memento*.

He is Leonard Shelby the ex-insurance investigator but he continually refuses the identity of 'Lenny', a name assigned by his dead wife, Catherine. He 'puts on' an identity that is constructed through the ownership of commodities such as a designer suit and Jaguar car, but this identity is taken through violent action, the killing of Jimmy Grantz, which is reconfigured as heroic revenge. Leonard borrows from the subcultural practices of self-tattooing to inscribe identity on his body in textual fragments, one of which asserts the patriarchal relations of marriage in the tattoo which includes the words, 'my wife', and through which he understands his relationship to Catherine whilst simultaneously denying her name. Each of these revisions to Leonard's identity can be accommodated within the discursive boundaries of the New Man and Retributive Man. However, due to his memory condition, Leonard, can never resolve them within one unified sense of self. As such the anterograde amnesia, the condition that stops Leonard from creating new memories, also inhibits the unification of his self-identity and in this sense a discourse of impairment is continually called on to rupture the desired coherence of masculinity. Cognitive impairment in this case invokes a disablement of masculinity whilst maintaining the presence of an embodied masculinity through the repeated display of Leonard and his tattoos, and in doing so offers a further example of *Memento*'s discursive dissonance, this time between mind and body.

Conclusion

The white male body is demonstrably present in constructions of masculinity and central to lifestyle practices such as personal grooming in the New Man discourse or as hyper-masculine spectacle in the discourse of the Retributive Man. In *film noir*, it is traditionally the female body that is displayed as the erotic object, exposed to the male gaze. Yet in *Memento*, Leonard's body is displayed on a number of occasions, when he undresses himself and when he is disrobed by Natalie, inviting careful and repeated contemplation. Leonard's passive display is contradicted by the tattooed messages on his body, which in themselves are, in the mode of the Retributive Man, a form of self-inflicted pain and masochistic suffering. *Memento* is not alone in depicting the spectacle of masochistic suffering of the white male body in the search for a coherent sense of masculinity: a similar theme underpins *Fight Club* (Fincher, 1999), which was released only a year prior to *Memento*. Leonard's self-tattooing parallels the self-inflicted injuries that the main protagonist causes by fighting with himself/Tyler and the splitting of identity is similarly delineated through the discourses of the New Man (Norton's character) and Retributive Man (Pitt's character). Masochistic suffering is configured in both films as necessary to the journey towards the resolution of identity. However, in *Memento* that coherence is never reached and whereas in *Fight Club* the split identities find resolution at the end of the film, in *Memento* identity is rendered ambiguous with little possibility of restitution. What is repeatedly disambiguated is Leonard's condition, which is not only explained within the dialogue but dominates the film's narrative structure, effectively leaning toward the 'tendency to position eccentric experience as intelligible within a dominant biomedical framework'.[24] One reason for this is suggested by Tom Shakespeare when he writes that the position between impairment and masculinity is untenable such that 'a disabled man is not able to conform to the cultural demands of masculinity and gender identity, yet to be accepted within society he must have an appropriate gender identity'.[25] What *Memento* may foreground then is an ongoing tension between different discourses of masculinity which are further troubled by the invocation of a discourse of impairment which, as yet, popular culture more generally has been unable to reconcile satisfactorily and assimilate into its understandings of masculinity.

5 So What Really Happened? *Memento*, Fans and Online Interpretive Strategies

The whole idea was to make a film that bled into the mind a little bit, spun in your head, that you constructed very much yourself.

Christopher Nolan[1]

Following *Memento*'s release Internet forums began to buzz with discussion about Christopher Nolan's second feature, and debates continued for many months as hypotheses about various aspects of the film multiplied. These forums played a major role in creating word of mouth, especially in the first months of release when posts to online discussion groups made repeated recommendations that people should not wait for the DVD release but see the film immediately. As one poster advised: 'Go see this film, drive to one of the select cities, it will be worth the ride.'[2] With *Memento* on limited release and opening predominantly on the art-house circuit in the US, many similar online posts recommended travelling to find the nearest art-house theatre where the film was playing. Given *Memento*'s limited marketing budget online word of mouth was to prove particularly valuable and, as box office returns suggested, also effective.

As the buzz about *Memento* grew, explanations about the film changed as material from the film's website, interviews, critical reviews and later from the DVD and Jonathan Nolan's short story were amalgamated into hypotheses and used to confirm or develop interpretations. On one discussion board a thread that started after the North American release began with a comment posted on 18 March 2001, which asked: 'What did everyone think about *Memento*'s ending?'[3] The following day and fourteen posts later another contributor said that they had found the film's website and posted the address, otnemem.com, for forum members. Whilst some contributors from the community visited the official site and incorporated the online material into their various hypotheses about Leonard and the film, others were less willing to integrate the website information. One contributor contended, 'I am going to stand by what I saw in the movie. I say: screw the website!'[4] What these responses illustrate is that somewhere between the imagined audience assumed by the marketing discourse and the ideal spectator presupposed by cognitive theory were the 'real' people who watched the film, visited the website, bought or rented the DVD, read reviews, participated in discussions about the film and generated word of mouth. It is the relationship between these activities with reference to the film which forms the focus of this chapter.

Online forums were, and continue to be, an important aspect of interpretive activity and part of a continuum of meaning-making. Alongside marketing communications and critical and scholarly responses to the film, user-generated content from Internet forums and message boards was involved in the production and shaping of discourses on *Memento*. Even a cursory glance at reported visitor figures to the Internet Movie Database, estimated at 57 million per month in 2009 and in excess of 18 million in 2001, points toward online communities having a meaningful role to play in popular discourse formation.[5] Although IMDb is a publicly accessible online film database it also fulfils certain criteria which classify it as a consumption-related online community. A recent study of word of mouth communication in online communities proposes the following description:

Consumption-related online communities essentially represent WOM [word of mouth] networks, where individuals with an interest in a product category interact for information such as purchase advice, to affiliate with other like-minded individuals, or to participate in complaint or compliment interactions.[6]

WOM is considered to have higher levels of credibility and trustworthiness than formal marketing communications due, in part, to a perception that the information is independent of the market and therefore less prone to bias. Moreover, assumed similarities in attitudes or interests will predispose individuals toward greater trust in WOM communication. Thus WOM exerts increased influence within both an offline context and in online communities. In this sense, a site such as IMDb can be regarded as an Internet community with a shared interest in film whose online interactions and activities, including WOM communication, contributed to the construction of discourses on *Memento*. This is not to say that IMDb was the only, or necessarily even the primary, locus of online word of mouth for *Memento*, but it was a crucial node within the discursive nexus. This point is underscored when one considers not only the monthly visitor traffic but also that the formal marketing communications exploited *Memento*'s ranking at the number twelve spot in the IMDb top 250 movies, using it within print advertisements for the film that appeared in the *Los Angeles Times* in June 2001.[7] This use of the film's ranking would suggest that such online recognition would have meaning which would be acknowledged by a wider film-going public.

This chapter then looks at the development of the public discourse as it was presented online, predominantly at IMDb but also from other discussion boards and newsgroups, in an attempt to establish how audiences responded to and made sense of *Memento* as both a narrative and a cultural product.[8] Examining these interpretive strategies suggests a dynamic relationship between audiences and films in which audiences are active in the process of meaning-making. This is not to suggest that the activity which audiences engage in excludes or overrides the import of discourses produced, for instance, by scholars, critics or filmmakers. Indeed, it is the dynamic of public participation in and negotiation with authorised discourses that is of interest. As such, this chapter draws on notions of taste, subculture and cultural capital to examine the public discourse and to identify where these ideas usefully intersect in relation to *Memento*.

IMDb and subcultural capital

In online communities greater emphasis is placed on shared interests than on shared socio-economic characteristics, whilst people tend to form weaker bonds compared to those in 'real-life' communities.[9] One reason for this is the relative ease with which people can enter and leave online communities. As Pippa Norris remarks, 'Most purely online communities without any physical basis are usually low-cost, "easy-entry, easy-exit" groups. To avoid cognitive dissonance, it is simpler to exit than to work through any messy bargaining and conflictual disagreements within the group.'[10] As a consequence, online activity in Internet communities produces fluid, flexible groupings around a vast and complex array of forms of cultural consumption. An Internet community, in this sense, is usefully described by Rhiannon Bury: 'What gives the community its substance is the consistent engagement of *communal practices* by a majority of its members.'[11] In this sense, Internet communities are not a fixed set of individuals but are composed of the outcomes of individuals' practices. Activity on IMDb is thus constituted by communal practices that include registered users posting comments, participation in discussion boards and their ratings of individual films.[12] Such communities are transient though, and activity coalesces, shifts and ebbs around particular films, constructing discourses about them and allocating value to them within hierarchical ranking systems, such as the IMDb top 250 movies, that reflect the performance of the community's dominant taste preferences. Whilst online communities are flexible in this way, the demographics of Internet and IMDb users are also useful in terms of providing some sense of which tastes are expressed and therefore dominant in this online sphere.

By the time of *Memento*'s US release, the gap between male and female Internet usage there had been eroded. Although studies in 1997 had shown that male Internet usage was higher than female, by 2001 the Internet use rate for males and females was equal (53.9 per cent and 53.8 per cent respectively).[13] Highest Internet usage was in the under-25 age group although female Internet usage was on average 4.2 per cent higher than male usage in the 20–50 age group and the likelihood of using the Internet increased the higher the level of educational attainment.[14] Among graduates at BA level and beyond Internet use in 2001 was 83.7 per cent compared, with 39.8 per cent among people with a high school diploma and 12.8 per cent among people whose educational level was classified as 'less than high school'.[15] Despite the apparent equivalence in gender presence online as suggested by the 2001 figures, on the IMDb ratings system for *Memento* the film was scored by nearly seven times more males than females, with the highest proportion of voters being in the 19–25 age group. This reflects the wider voting trend across IMDb where the male/female ratios of user ratings for the top ten films in the IMDb top 250 movies remains between 6:1 and 10:1. The largest proportion of IMDb users have a Bachelor Degree which accords with similar levels of Internet usage in the wider population in 2001, and whilst IMDb comments have a substantially higher proportion of male input this disparity may not necessarily be the case with the gender ratios of people accessing the comments or the site in general. Nonetheless, it is reasonable to propose that in 2001, although fluid in its composition, the dominant tastes expressed by the IMDb community in user comments and through the ratings system which ranks the top 250 films were those of well-educated North American males under the age of 25. It is notable that this does not correspond with the assumed audience for independent films – 'upscale, educated' consumers 'aged twenty-five to forty-five'[16] – but does align with the college audience targeted by *Memento*'s marketing campaign.

IMDb user comments on *Memento* formed an experiential consumption 'word of mouth network' through which the tastes of individuals were expressed whilst the ranking system and IMDb top 250 reflected the dominant tastes of the community, which have in turn kept *Memento* in the top twenty films since 2001. According to Pierre Bourdieu, taste is a system of classificatory schemes which can be mapped onto social groups and to these ends:

> Taste, the propensity and capacity to appropriate (materially or symbolically) a given class of classified, classifying objects or practices, is the generative formula of lifestyle, a unitary set of distinctive preferences which expresses the same expressive intention in the specific logic of each of the symbolic sub-spaces . . ..[17]

Bourdieu argues that the unity of taste functions to mark out boundaries of social stratification through practices of symbolic consumption. The consumption of cultural goods is, however, uneven and, Bourdieu suggests, dominant classes accrue the greatest levels of economic and cultural capital. Accumulation of cultural capital (which includes education) is, he argues, as significant as the accumulation of economic capital, and aesthetic attitudes become a means of distinction between classes. Given the dominant level of educational attainment of IMDb users there is clearly a case to be made here that the tastes expressed in IMDb comments about *Memento* were those of a social group with a high degree of cultural capital. However, contemporary destabilisation and fragmentation of mass identities has given way to much looser, flexible and mobile affiliations. Thus whilst Bourdieu's observations on taste and cultural capital are useful when thinking critically about the broad groups of Internet and IMDb users, his emphasis on the maintenance of fixed underlying class boundaries is less applicable when considering the activities in online communities. Moreover, the practices of groups that form around and comment on particular films on IMDb and other online message boards bear closer parallels with existing conceptions of fan subcultures than with larger forms of social stratification such as class.

In her development of Bourdieu's work, Sarah Thornton (1995) argues that class is less relevant as a means of distinction within subcultures where tastes are defined against a mainstream which is, in turn, constructed as 'Other', in order for individuals to accrue status through 'subcultural capital'.[18] Thornton's notion of subculture is relevant here as discourses which emerge from online postings often coalesce around the positioning of *Memento* in relation to 'the mainstream' as well as legitimising distinctions between 'average movie goers', unintelligent and intelligent spectators, and those with the capacities to appreciate Nolan's film. Those writing about *Memento* in online communities often invoke a monolithic 'mainstream' as a self-evident 'reality' against which taste preferences and values can be measured as a means of policing the boundaries of such distinctions. The oppositional binary is far from stable though and disagreements among individuals in a community such as IMDb demonstrate multiple appropriations of 'mainstream', 'indie' and 'independent'. In terms of defining a fan, Henry Jenkins' proposal that a person is a fan, 'not by being a regular viewer of a particular program but by translating that viewing into some type of cultural activity, by sharing feelings and thoughts about the program content with friends, by joining a community of other fans who share common interests'[19] has resonance for this discussion. Moreover, Janet Staiger's comments that fan interpretive communities will seek to resolve textual contradictions and place 'different weight on certain forms of evidence or reading'[20] becomes particularly salient with regard to *Memento*'s intentional ambiguity and narrative complexity.

Between Hollywood, art house and indie

Both critical and public responses to *Memento* unsurprisingly focused predominantly on the reverse ordered narrative, giving rise to questions about whether the alternative structure was justified, an unwarranted yoking of art-house conventions to a genre film or merely a gimmick. In response, the 'authorised' discourse promulgated through published critical reviews was remarkably consistent. A *Sunday Times* review opined. 'In theory it's a pretentious piece of twaddle. . . . it sounds like an art-house Michael Winner film staring Charles Bronson and scripted by Alain Robbe-Grillet. But in fact this great little movie is an entertaining enigma [. . .]'.[21]Another review published following the film's screening at the Venice Film Festival stated: 'It all sounds like a recipe for high-concept pretension, but the narrative tension is maintained expertly throughout and the end result is gripping and intellectually satisfying'.[22] Elsewhere critics noted that *Memento* 'is never for a moment smug or condescending'[23] and that the film 'avoids pretension through cool self-irony'.[24] Critical responses positioned *Memento* within a discourse of intelligent filmmaking and justified the film's appropriation of alternative conventions more usually associated with art house as an intriguing and innovative device that set the film apart from the usual mainstream offerings with one reviewer going so far as to say that *Memento* 'spits at Hollywood convention'.[25] Critical responses revealed an implicit, and sometime explicit, alignment of art house with pretension, and positioned *Memento* as a film able to defy Hollywood conventions, associated with formulaic filmmaking, without succumbing to art house self-importance. The majority of reviews that commented on *Memento*'s liminal location outside Hollywood and art house did not, however, relate this position to independence. In this sense the implied 'freedom' that Nolan enjoyed to make *Memento* in defiance of traditional conventions was not linked in critical reviews to the film's independent status.

The Internet Movie Database user comments revealed an interesting negotiation of identity for the film between Hollywood, indie and art house. Responses to the film on the online public review board suggested that those who had seen *Memento* felt that it was being wrongly restricted to the art house circuit. These comments represented a groundswell of opinion that *Memento* deserved a wider release to achieve public recognition, although significantly many qualified their point with a statement that 'other people', those more used to mainstream cinema, would not understand it. Moreover, the topic of *Memento*, positioned as a non-mainstream film, voiced criticisms about theatrical distribution practices and the Academy of Motion Picture Arts and Sciences, both of which were considered to be oriented primarily towards a mass film culture, which was regularly described in posts as 'formulaic' and 'mind-numbing'. Typical of such comments, one newsgroup post stated:

Don't get me wrong, it's my favorite movie this year, but the Oscars have a way of missing the gems and instead picking movies that are part good/part popular. With a movie making only $10.1M as of this week (so says imdb), the Oscar 'judges' would rather fill it with movies that brought in the money . . . I mean, people. Look for *Memento* to pass under the radar screen of most people except for those who actively look for non-Hollywood-formula movies instead of what's the coolest, most played commercial.[26]

Although the film was broadly regarded as different from mainstream film, more often referred to collectively as 'Hollywood', criticisms of the film's release pattern implied resistance to the notion that *Memento* was 'art house'. Given the public perception of *Memento* as outside both art house and commercial cinema, it is interesting that there was little mention of the film's independent status. From the 1,500 user comments posted at IMDb about *Memento* between 9 September 2000 and 24 July 2004, only sixteen identified the film as 'independent' and seven as 'indie', representing just 1.5 per cent of total user comments.[27] The responses that did mention independence or indie in some register tended to regard the terms in relation to a particular aesthetic, using terms such 'gritty', 'rough', 'unpolished' and 'edgy'. The film's independent identity and style were also challenged, suggesting that *Memento* was a mainstream film disguised as an indie, having high production values and a Hollywood feel that masqueraded as art house. Responses such as these suggested that spectators maintained a sense of authentic independence or 'real indie' which they felt able to identify and, significantly, that they understood could be co-opted by a mainstream system. These posts also revealed an interesting negotiation of independence which relied less on economic determinants and instead privileged a particular 'indie style'.

In discussions of film style 3.7 per cent of the 1,500 IMDb comments used the terms 'art', 'arty', 'artsy' or 'artistic' when referring to *Memento* and when trying to locate a place for it within a mainstream/alternative binary. Users expressed the sense that *Memento* occupied a space between Hollywood and art which made it accessible to a wider audience whilst not becoming either formulaic or too 'artsy'. References to the film being 'art', 'artsy' and 'artistic' could feature as both disparagement and praise. Where the film was referred to as art, this was most commonly related to notions of quality, complexity and intelligent filmmaking. Although in the minority, negative comments associated 'art' with difficulty, leading such posts to consider *Memento* an impenetrable text. The rest of the comments that included some reference to art in the pejorative sense associated it with pretension.

The peculiarities of *Memento*'s narrative structure were central to these discussions where the reverse ordering was hotly debated, giving rise to arguments that emphasised, on the one hand, the originality of the film in contrast to criticisms that it was 'gimmicky' on the other hand. In one newsgroup a contributor wrote: 'the tactic felt like an independent film gimmick and kept reminding me that I was watching a gimmicky independent film'.[28] IMDb user comments echoed this sentiment, claiming that the 'gimmick', or reverse ordered narrative, was the element that enabled the film to masquerade as cool indie. Although the term 'gimmick' occurred frequently in relation to *Memento*, the word appearing 153 times in IMDb user comments, it was not necessarily always applied pejoratively – many comments defended the use of the backward plotting claiming that its contribution to the overall film experience warranted its application. As such, comments that regarded the reverse ordered narrative as a gimmick tended to consider the backward narrative as innovative or otherwise articulated a level of distrust towards the film, deeming it to be too clever in the sense that it utilised a gimmick to deceive people into believing that it was intelligent filmmaking.

Memento was described as 'intelligent', 'clever' or 'smart' in 15.5 per cent of the IMDb user comments. Many of the posts used the terms as indicators of quality and made comparisons between *Memento*'s intelligence and the lack of it in the majority of commercial films. On this comparison one newsgroup post stated: 'I challenge someone to watch *Memento* and then try to defend shallow action films. *Memento* makes you realize how ripped off we are by other films.'[29] 'Intelligent' was also used as a way of identifying a particular type of filmgoer and many posts articulated a clear division between intelligent people who could watch *Memento* and those who were unable to sit through the film. This demarcation did not necessarily only represent a difference among people who understood the film but among those who were able to watch it in the way demanded by the film, that is, with a high level of concentration and the ability to maintain focus, and those who could not. These posts articulated an imposed differentiation between groups of filmgoers as well as a reflexive self-identification with a community of spectators able to meet the levels of concentration demanded by narrative complexity and as a consequence derive pleasure from making sense of the text.

Critical communities

Within online forums, those who appreciated the film constituted a critical community and *Memento* enabled a particular form of discursive positioning through which individuals emphasised certain features of the film – for instance, intelligence, intellectual engagement, artistic expression and complexity – which located it outside mainstream commercial cinema and beyond the grasp of the 'average movie-goer'. The practice of watching, understanding and deriving pleasure from the film was thus constructed as an interpretive activity which set apart those who under-stood *Memento* from a mainstream audience. The identity of *Memento* enthusiasts was constructed through a negotiation of the otherness of mainstream audiences and necessarily invoked over-generalisations about 'average movie-goers' to reinforce the differentiation. As such, the construction of a general mass of 'average movie-goers' who lacked intel-ligence, concentration and an appreciation of complexity was essential to establishing a coherent identity for *Memento* fans. Those who wished to make negative comments about the film therefore had to negotiate a position that allowed them to claim legitimacy within the critical com-munity whilst not being categorised as one of the 'masses who don't understand'. This tended to be resolved by asserting certain credentials, such as claiming the identity of an intelligent filmgoer, a cinephile or being a fan of another film – either an art-house film or one with a higher IMDb ranking. Moreover, disbelief was expressed by fans about those who maintained that they had fully understood the film or who claimed that they had no need for repeat viewings to appreciate its complexity fully. In response to such comments one forum post argued:

Sure, everyone gets 'the basics' that's why they are basic. I wanted to understand everything. The director did certain things on purpose so that the audience would barely get it, or miss it completely . . . that's probably where you are getting your 'plot holes'. It's a complete story once you get it. Try it a second time, I gaurentee [*sic*], you missed something.[30]

For fans the ambiguity, 'working out', multiple viewings and discus-sion with other forum members were part of the pleasures of the text and constituted a set of practices associated with the consumption of puzzle movies. Films that necessitated such practices were constructed as 'intelligent' whilst also conferring the same status on those who pursued detailed explanations or close readings. Thus, posts about the film also commented on the amount of 'work' required to make sense of *Memento* in comparison to the ease with which a mainstream or Hollywood film was understood.

The preference for *Memento* expressed by spectators presupposed a set of values external to their personal tastes. Such values were organ-ised into a discursive hierarchy where intelligence and complexity were equated with quality. Being inaccessible to a large audience due to its complexity rather than because of its limited release and then being overlooked at the 2002 Oscars legitimated the film's standing and further confirmed the authority of the value system expressed through the critical discourse. To garner mass appeal would undermine the intelligent status of the film and when *Memento* received only two Oscar nominations the perceived rejection by the Academy, which was constructed as an arbiter of mass tastes, was easily negotiated by and integrated into the critical discourse.[31] In a general discussion about nominations one post noted: 'I am definitely not watching the Oscars this year. Way to celebrate mediocrity! Where's *Memento* for Best Picture?'[32] On Internet forums fans asserted that they were pleased that the film had not won any awards as this would have opened it up to a mass audience who lacked the capacity to appreciate it and the Academy awards were constructed as having little concern for films with small marketing budgets. The Academy was located within a product-driven marketplace which was in turn designed to appeal to the mainstream. This construction was important within the discourse on *Memento* as the Oscars represented a particular value system that, once it had overlooked *Memento*, necessarily had to be aligned with poor taste and average filmgoers who 'did not understand'.

Another strategy used to validate *Memento*'s difference from mainstream film was to make comparisons with other films. This was a particularly important aspect of the discourse and although the terms 'unique' and 'original' were used to describe the film on 182 and 368 occasions respectively in IMDb comments, reviews tended to group *Memento* with other films of similar perceived quality, aesthetic, themes and structure. The films most frequently used for comparison were *Pulp Fiction*, *Sixth Sense*, *Fight Club* and *The Usual Suspects*, all of which can be categorised with *Memento* as puzzle films. Positive public reviews typically pointed to similarities in terms of going against mainstream norms or Hollywood conventions, temporal reorganisation, having an unexpected 'twist' and being refreshing, different or unique. Negative comments also typically invoked these films in unfavourable comparisons, particularly with regard to the reverse ordered narrative. Three of the comparison films – *Pulp Fiction*, *Fight Club* and *The Usual Suspects* – were consistently ranked in the top 30 films on the IMDb top 250 movies and as such were established within the wider IMDb community as a benchmark of quality. *The Sixth Sense*, on the other hand, had a lower ranking on the IMDb top 250 and tended to be less well accepted as a film that was comparable to *Memento*.

Comparisons between *Memento* and other films were contested among IMDb users when they were translated into rankings on the IMDb top

250 movies. In mid-April 2001 *Memento* was ranked at number 56 but by early June 2001 it had moved to twelfth position, which was subsequently exploited in the film's marketing and used in print adverts published in the *Los Angeles Times*. Three months later *Memento* was just outside the top ten (at number 11) but had moved to ninth at the end of September. It stayed there until the end of January 2002 when it dropped one place, eventually slipping to number 12 on the top 250 movies list in June 2003. With an overall 8.5 out of a maximum 10 rating and being ranked higher than films such as *Fight Club* (number 31), *Taxi Driver* (Scorsese, 1976) (number 27), *Pulp Fiction* (19), *Usual Suspects* (15) and *Rear Window* (14) in 2001, *Memento*'s position raised much debate among the IMDb community. Some users expressed surprise at seeing a film at number 12 that they had not heard of before and stated that they went to see *Memento* because of its high ranking and recommendations from other IMDb users. From June 2001 the debate about the film's ranking on IMDb became heated when users questioned whether the film deserved its place on the list and if the ranking accurately reflected the tastes of the IMDb community. At the core of this concern was the question of what constituted the authentic taste preferences of the online community. Moreover, where it was suggested that the preferences were those of 'untypical' members, self-identified 'authentic' users proposed that 'inauthentic posts' had the potential to undermine the credibility of the whole community. Woven into concerns about which taste preferences were emerging as dominant was an implicit discourse of community rules of interpretation and classification.

Conclusion

Despite not being of acknowledged as an independent film within critical or public discourses at the time, *Memento* is now recognised as an exemplification of twenty-first-century indie filmmaking. The film's reverse narrative structure and Christopher Nolan's directorial mastery have been elevated to the level of the essentialised features of *Memento*, conceived of within an independent filmmaking framework. The emphasis on these characteristics has necessarily subordinated other aspects of the film which, under a different set of circumstances, might have been brought to the fore. For instance, Nolan's hyphenate status as writer-director not only of *Memento* but also *Doodlebug, Following, Batman Begins, The Prestige* and *The Dark Knight* has generated little interest when compared to the recognition of his strictly directorial achievements. Similarly when *Memento* was released, the casting of Carrie-Anne Moss and Joe Pantoliano who had recently starred in one of the top grossing films of 1999, *The Matrix*, received remarkably little attention in comparison to the ongoing fascination with *Memento*'s purposeful ambiguity in both critical and public discussions of the film. Beyond the trade press, Newmarket had little impact on public awareness of the film, a point demonstrated by the fact that the company was mentioned only once in 1,500 IMDb user comments posted online. Whereas major independents such as Miramax and New Line Cinema carved out a marketable identity as independent distributors, despite Newmarket's success with *Memento* and a clutch of other indie films, there was scant acknowledgement of the company in public consciousness. Although Nolan was acclaimed for his innovatieness, artistry and narrative risk-taking, it is fair to say that the financial risk was Newmarket's.

Whilst the film's independent status found little recognition, the discourses on *Memento* constantly invoked the 'mainstream' in an opposition that aligned the film, albeit implicitly, with characteristics that were intrinsically tied to notions of independence. In this sense, what was broadly conceived of as 'Hollywood' and its imagined mainstream/ multiplex audience offered a way of positioning *Memento* as an intelligent, cool, edgy and innovative alternative to what was perceived of as formulaic fodder for an undiscerning and unintellingent 'average filmgoer'. What is particularly interesting about this negotiation of *Memento*'s status is that whilst 'mainstream' had more significance in establishing *Memento*'s difference from Hollywood films, 'independence' in turn has gathered more symbolic weight when articulated within later discourses of studio filmmaking. This shift has been precipitated by the move of the new wave of independent directors into studio filmmaking. They include Nolan with the *Batman* franchise, Bryan Singer (*X-Men*) and Sam Raimi (*Spider-Man*). The indie/*auteur* status of these directors is particularly valued in terms of 'serious' filmmaking credibility, a particular aesthetic vision and the ability to bring an independent sensibility to studio filmmaking. As one article stated: 'the studios have recognized a need for spicier flavors and are much more willing to let folks who made their name on the fringes take a shot at bringing their tastes to the masses.'[33] In this sense, there is a continued emphasis in both independent and mainstream filmmaking on producing films that find a balance between commercial appeal and independent credibility.

Christopher Nolan has negotiated this balance strategically, claiming to be a 'mainstream director' during the marketing of *Memento* and an 'independent' when filming *Batman Begins* and *The Dark Knight*. It is significant to note, however, that the audience for *Memento* persistently ignored Nolan's claims to be a mainstream director, as did the critical reviews of the film, preferring to concentrate on his refreshingly innovative and intelligent approach. Claims to both commercial and indie identities are more than just clever manoeuvring on Nolan's part though, as he has managed to bridge the indie/commercial gap with psychologically complex characters, a distinctive neo-*noir* aesthetic and engagement with narrative complexity, coupled with adherence to aspects of mainstream film, such as a three-act structure and familiar generic tropes. In this way, Nolan has managed to bring complexity, innovation and the *auteur* vision of an independent director to his work without alienating mainstream audiences. *Memento* stands as testament to this, and whilst there may be no resolution to Leonard's identity crisis, the film itself profits both economically and aesthetically from occupying the dual identities of commercially viable and independently visionary.

Notes

Introduction

1. '"Memento": Not "Too Smart" for Profits', *Los Angeles Times*, 7 2001.
2. See Anthony Kaufman (2001) 'PARK CITY 2001: David vs. Goliath, Small Films Battle Industry Heavyweights in Competition', *indieWire*, 19 January 2001, online http://www.indiewire.com/onthescene/ fes_01Sund_010119_Day1.html (accessed 24 July 2008).
3. Jacques Thelemaque, quoted in Timothy Rhys (2003) 'Why Independent Film is Alive and Well', *MovieMaker*, 2 May 2003, online at http://www. moviemaker.com / directing / article / why _ independent _ film _ is _ alive_and_well_3264/ (accessed 10 December 2008).
4. Yannis Tzioumakis offers a comprehensive account of American independent cinema as a set of discourses. See especially Tzioumakis (2006a), pp. 8–12.
5. *Filmmaker* is the magazine of Independent Feature Project (IFP), a network of non-profit organisations that promote independent film and filmmakers. See http://www.ifp.org/.
6. *Filmmaker*, 'The Fifty Most Important Independent Films', Fall 1996, Vol. 5, No. 1, p. 40.
7. Ibid.
8. Ibid.
9. *Empire*, 'The Fifty Greatest Independent Films: Empire's Ultimate Indie Line-up' posted online at http://www.empireonline.com/ features/50greatestindependent/ (accessed 30 July 2009).
10. This list is updated. Film listings quoted here are correct as of July 2009.
11. Correct as of March 2009.
12. *Empire*, 'The Fifty Greatest Independent Films: Empire's Ultimate Indie Line-up', posted online at http://www.empireonline.com/ features/50greatestindependent/ (accessed 30 July 2009).

13. 'The Dark Knight', *Variety.com*, 6 July 2008, online at http://www.variety.com/review/VE1117937619.html?categoryid=3266&cs=1 (accessed 30 July 2009); Kotler, 2006 online at http://www.variety.com/awardcentral_vstory/VR1117935961.html (accessed 3 August 2009).
14. Kotler (2006), online at http://www.variety.com/awardcentral_vstory/VR1117935961.html (accessed 3 August 2009).
15. 'Nolan Brings Indie Sensibility to "Knight": Director Makes Batman Films Deeper, Moodier', *Variety.com*, 10 May 2008, online at http://www.variety.com/article/VR1117982193.html?categoryid=2181&cs=1 (accessed 30 July 2009).
16. In 2008, *The Dark Knight* became the second highest grossing film of all time, behind *Titanic* (Cameron, 1997).
17. With some notable exceptions (for example, Tzioumakis, 2006a), the speed with which independent companies emerge and are subsequently acquired or go out of business has led to a paucity of 'indie' micro-histories, with the majority of scholarly work being focused on successful major independents which have achieved some measure of longevity, such as Miramax.
18. Jenkins (1992), p. 5.

Chapter 1

1. Interview with William Tyrer and Christopher Ball, quoted in Amy Wallace (2000) 'No Fame Please, Just Go See Our Pictures', *Los Angeles Times*, 19 2000, pp. F2 and F17.
2. Box office figures taken from www.imdb.com
3. Bob Weinstein is quoted in Biskind (2007) as saying about *sex, lies, and videotape*: 'That's the best title I've ever heard. That title alone will sell the movie.' Biskind comments, 'From a marketing point of view, just the fact that it contained the word "sex" was golden' (Biskind, 2007, p. 64). See also Wyatt (1998), pp. 79–81.
4. Biskind (2007), p. 144. For an account of the marketing strategy for *The Crying Game*, see ibid., pp. 142–9.
5. Richard Corliss and Elizabeth Bland, 'Don't Read This Story', *Time Magazine*, 1 March 1993, online at http://www.time.com/time/magazine/article/0,9171,977831,00.html (accessed 8 December 2008).
6. Wyatt (1998), p. 81. However, Miramax initially considered the Academy award nomination for Jaye Davidson as Best Supporting Actor for *The*

Crying Game problematic as it revealed that Davidson was in fact male and thus divulged the 'secret' of the film.

7. For instance, Justin Wyatt notes that 'Repeatedly, Miramax has maximized the publicity created by challenging the MPAA ratings system' (Wyatt, 1998, p. 80).
8. Biskind (2007), p. 191.
9. See Groves (1993), online http://www.variety.com/article/VR103897. html?categoryid=18&cs=1 (accessed 8 December 2008).
10. Jay Green (1994) 'Battered, but Still Standing', *Variety.com*, 25 February 1994, online http://www.variety.com/index.asp?layout=print_story& articleid=VR118621&categoryid=18 (accessed 29 July 2008).
11. See *Variety.com*, http://www.variety.com/article/VR1116676611.html? categoryid=18&cs=1&query=completion+bond (accessed 29 July 2008).
12. Holmlund and Wyatt (2005), p. 7.
13. http://www.variety.com/article/VR1117490524. html?cs=1&query=slamdance+1999 (accessed 29 July 2008).
14. For data and discussion of the potential revenues created by Oscar nominations, see Randy Nelson and Doug Atchison, 'The Economics of the Oscars', *MovieMaker*, 7 January 2003, online at http://www. moviemaker.com/directing/article/the_economics_of_oscar_3011/ (accessed 24 July 2008).
15. Box office figure from *Box Office Mojo* 'The Oscar Boost' at http://www. boxofficemojo.com/oscar/bestpichist.htm?view=bymovie&p=.htm (accessed 24 July 2008).
16. Biskind (2007), p. 151.
17. King (2005), pp. 42–3.
18. Miramax's acquisition strategy eventually culminated in the company paying a reported $11 million for *Happy Texas* (Illsley, 1999) at Sundance in 1999. See Bing (2001), p. 51.
19. See Hopwell (2002), online http://www.variety.com/article/ VR1117874420.html?categoryid=1336&cs=1 (accessed 24 July 2008).
20. See Khan (2002), online http://www.variety.com/article/ VR1117874422.html?categoryid=1336&cs=1 (accessed 24 July 2008).
21. Worldwide grosses for *The Passion of the Christ* taken from 'Indie Power 50' in *Hollywood Reporter*, 17 January 2008. Also *Boxofficemojo.com*, online http://boxofficemojo.com/movies/?id=passionofthechrist.htm (accessed 24 July 2008).
22. Mike Goodridge (2004) 'Newmarket in the Limelight', *Screen International*, 7 May 2004, p. 10.

23. Jay Green (1994) 'Ex-Daiwa Exex Open Loan Biz', *Variety.com*, 3 March 1994, online http://www.variety.com/article/VR118829. html?categoryid=18&cs=1 (accessed 28 July 2008).
24. See Grove (1998), pp. A4 and A12.
25. Ibid., p. A12.
26. Budget and gross for *Dead Man* taken from *IMDb.com*. See http://www. imdb.com/title/tt0112817/business (accessed 28 July 2008).
27. Mike Goodridge (1998) 'Artisan Reaches for Summit' *Screen International*, 17 April 1998.
28. Wallace (2000), p. F17.
29. See Carver (1999), pp. 1 and 26.
30. Wallace (2000), p. F2.
31. Mottram (2005), p. 177.
32. Jonathan Nolan described his idea for a short story to his brother during a car journey. The original short story was later written by Jonathan, titled *Memento Mori* and published in *Esquire* magazine.
33. New Wave also supported Nolan and *Following* with a marketing strategy, which included festival screenings, to secure North American distribution.
34. See *Time Out*, 3 November 1999.
35. Mottram (2002), p. 124.
36. Leonard's looser narration was shot after the film's official wrap
37. Elvis Mitchell (2003) 'Cannes Film Festival: Trading War Stories in Cannes' Doldrums', *The New York Times*, 22 May 2003, online at http://query. nytimes.com/gst/fullpage.html?res=9E07EFDA1E3EF931A15756C0A 9659C8B63&sec=&spon=&pagewanted=2 (accessed 28 July 2008).
38. Joe Pantoliano also appeared in *The Matrix* but did not achieve the same bankable star status as Carrie-Ann Moss.
39. Mottram (2002), p. 51.
40. Ibid.
41. All figures taken from *IMDb.com* from weekend box office data supplied by ACNielsen EDI.
42. Limited release refers here to a film that has theatrical release in fewer than 600 theatres. All figures for the period January 2001 to July 2001 from *Variety*, 16 July 2001.
43. Revenue figures from *Hollywood Reporter*, 25 October 2001 and *Home Media Magazine*, 18 January 2002.
44. Pay TV licence fee details from *Variety*, 22 March, 2002.
45. William Tyrer, quoted in Harris and Lyons (2002), p. 38.
46. Hesmondhalgh (2008), p. 92 (emphasis in original).

47. Ibid., p. 176.
48. It is salient to note (as Hesmondhalgh does) that in the case of film, interdependent webs have been operating for many decades. However, these have been under other economic and political conditions. See Tzioumakis (2006a), who details the various relationships between independents and majors and includes, for instance, prestige and low-end independent production during the studio era.

Chapter 2

1. 'Indie Angst', *New Times Los Angeles*, 15–21 March 2001, p. 16.
2. Bob Berney, quoted in '"Memento": Not "Too Smart" for Profits', *Los Angeles Times*, 7 May 2001.
3. See King (2005), pp. 48–9.
4. '"Memento": Not "Too Smart" for Profits,' *Los Angeles Times*, 7 May 2001.
5. William Tyrer, quoted in *Entertainment Weekly*, 30 March 2001, online at http://www.ew.com/ew/article/0,,103696,00.html (accessed 4 January 2009).
6. Mottram (2002), pp. 49–51.
7. 'Steven Soderbergh Unleashed' *Film Threat*, 25 March 2001, online at http://www.filmthreat.com/index.php?section=interviews&Id=125 (accessed 4 January 2009).
8. 'Indie Film is Dead', *Filmmaker*, Fall 1995, online at http://www.filmmakermagazine.com/fall1995/dead_film.php (accessed 4 January 2009).
9. Ibid.
10. See 'Survival of the Leanest', *Variety*, 25 July 2001, online at http://www.variety.com/article/VR1117850244.html?categoryid=1013&cs=1&query=limited+release+cost+1994 (accessed March 2009).
11. 'Indie Film is Dead'.
12. Levy (1999), p. 214.
13. Figures taken from the Motion Picture Association of America survey, reported in 'Film Marketing Savvy Shapes, Shakes Indies', *Variety*, 17 August 1993, online at http://www.variety.com/article/VR109679.html?categoryid=13&cs=1 (accessed 8 December 2008).
14. Advertising costs taken from Andrea Adelson (1993) 'Advertising: For its Latest Golden Age, Radio Has Recast Itself to Advertisers as the Home Of Niche Markets', *New York Times*, 28 December 1993, online at http://query.nytimes.com/gst/fullpage.html?res=9F0CE4DB1F3FF93BA15751C1A965958260 (accessed 6 January 2009).

15. 'Film Marketing Savvy Shapes, Shakes Indies'.
16. Figures from Hope (1995), online at http://www.filmmakermagazine. com/fall1995/dead_film.php (accessed 4 January 2009).
17. Dana and Ivers interview in *Variety*, 8 December 1993, online at http:// www.variety.com / article / VR116385.html?categoryid = 18&cs = 1& query=triton (accessed 4 January 2009).
18. 'Triton Distribbery Folds', *Variety*, 8 December 1993, online at http://www. variety.com / article / VR116385.html?categoryid = 18&cs = 1&query =triton (accessed 4 January 2009).
19. Justin Wyatt notes that Miramax's and New Line's affiliations and greater access to funds polarised the market for independent films (Wyatt, 1998, p. 84).
20. Kunz (2007), p. 122.
21. See 'Arthouse Chains Making Inroads', *Variety*, 24 July 1997 online at http:// www.variety.com / article / VR1116676622.html?categoryid = 13&cs=1 &query=arthouse+chains (accessed 4 January 2009).
22. Adelson, 'Advertising: For its Latest Golden Age, Radio Has Recast Itself to Advertisers as the Home of Niche Markets'.
23. 'Film Marketing Savvy Shapes, Shakes Indies'.
24. See: Adelson, Andrea (1993) 'Advertising: For its latest golden age, radio has recast itself to advertisers as the home of niche markets' in *New York Times*, December 28th 1993 online at http://query.nytimes.com/ gst/fullpage.html?res=9F0CE4DB1F3FF93BA15751C1A965958260 (accessed 6th January 2009).
25. Wyatt (1994), p. 96.
26. See Biskind (2007), p. 140.
27. Tyrer, quoted in Harris and Lyons (2002), p. 38.
28. Wyatt (2005), p. 243.
29. Sundance website http://www.sundance.org/press_subgen.html?article ID=1&colorCode=red (accessed 4 January 2009).
30. Often the marketing of the film author is secondary to the film. As Tzioumakis argues, independent marketing strategies 'tend to fore-ground first the independent "spirit and status" of the film and then any information about the film's author' (Tzioumakis, 2006b, p. 61).
31. King (2005), p. 11.
32. 'Following up', *Village Voice*, 13 April 1999.
33. See Kleinhans (1998), pp. 309-11.
34. Broderick (1993), online http://www.filmmakermagazine.com/ winter1993/film_for_song.php (accessed 4 January 2009).

35. Corliss and Harbison (1993), online http://www.time.com/time/maga-zine/article/0,9171,977898,00.html (accessed 4 January 2009).
36. *MovieMaker* (1994), online http://www.moviemaker.com/directing/article/kevin_smith_clerks_scott_mosier_20080908/ (accessed 4 January 2009).
37. See, for example, Timothy Rhys (2003) 'Why Independent Film is Alive and Well', *MovieMaker*, 2 May 2003, online at http://www.mov-iemaker.com/directing/article/why_independent_film_is_alive_and_well_3264/ (accessed 10 December 2008).
38. Moran and Willis, (1998), p. 22.
39. Martesko (1996) p. 4.
40. Moran and Willis (1998), p. 22.
41. Lucia and Porton (1999), p. 1.
42. West and West (1999), p. 28.
43. Moran and Willis (1998), p. 22.
44. See ibid.
45. Initial p&a costs were reported as $1.5 million and were later estimated to have increased to $25 million to include the re-release of the film in October 1999. See *Los Angeles Times*, 20 August 1999.
46. Wallace (1999), p. F1.
47. Berry (1999), p. 82.
48. According to Mottram (2002), Jonathan Nolan first worked with a friend, Marko Andrus, on the website. The site was then set up by Electric Artists in July 2001.
49. *Memento* website www.otnemem.com (accessed 4 January 2009).
50. Nolan, quoted in Mottram (2002), pp. 72–3.
51. Nolan, quoted in '"Memento": Not "Too Smart" for Profits'.
52. BBC interview with Christopher Nolan, 16 October 2000, online at http://www.bbc.co.uk/films/2000/10/16/christopher_nolan_i_inter-view.shtml (accessed, 4 January 2009).
53. Memento advertisement in *Time Out: London*, 18 October 2000.
54. Will Tyrer, quoted in '"Memento": Not 'Too Smart' for Profits'.
55. Tzioumakis (2009), p. 58.
56. Mottram (2002), p. 57.
57. Interview with Jonathan and Christopher Nolan, *All Things Considered*, 7 April 2001.
58. *Washington Post*, 4 June 2006, p.1, online at http://www.washingtonpost.com/wp-dyn/content/article/2006/06/02/AR2006060200344.html (accessed 4 January 2009).

59. *Screen International*, 30 January 2004, p. 12.
60. Nancarrow, Nancarrow and Page, 2001, p. 315.
61. Ibid., p. 311.

Chapter 3

1. Christopher Nolan, quoted in *New York Times*, 25 February 2001, p. 23.
2. Viewing figures taken from 'Hollywood Journal', *Wall Street Journal*, 11 May 2001.
3. Christopher Nolan interview for IFC (2001) on *Memento* Special Edition DVD 2004.
4. *Memento* Production Notes, 2001.
5. Christopher Nolan interview for IFC (2001) on *Memento* Special Edition DVD 2004.
6. Berg (2006), p. 56
7. Bordwell (2008), p. 33.
8. Buckland (2009), p. 6.
9. Ibid., p. 11.
10. Berg (2006), p. 8.
11. Ibid., p. 27.
12. Bordwell (2006), pp. 72–6.
13. Ibid., pp. 72–3.
14. Ibid., p. 72.
15. Elsaesser (2009), p. 19.
16. Berg argues that 'Tarantino's "wild" techniques are probably the most visible influence on unorthodox film narration' (Berg, 2006, p. 6). Bordwell (2006, p. 73) also notes that *Pulp Fiction* was an early example of the trend toward 'tricky storytelling' and Elliot Panek (2006) regards *Pulp Fiction* and *Blue Velvet* (Lynch, 1986, p. 65) as important films that immediately precede a growing tendency toward narrative ambiguity and unmotivated temporal shifts.
17. Berg (2006), p. 57.
18. Elsaesser (2009), pp. 38–9.
19. Tarantino, quoted in Murphy (2007), p. 143.
20. For an account of narrative complexity in American television entertainment, see Mittell (2006).
21. See Staiger (2006), p. 2; Berg (2006), pp. 6–7; Bordwell (2006), p. 73; Murphy (2007), p. 6.
22. Bordwell (2008), p. 150.

23. Ibid., p. 150.
24. Ibid., pp. 151–2.
25. Branigan (1992), p. 13.
26. Bordwell (2008), p. 156.
27. Ibid., p. 159.
28. Ibid.; Thompson (1999).
29. Thompson (1999), pp. 21–7.
30. Ibid., p. 28.
31. Bordwell (2006), p. 41.
32. Ibid., p. 206.
33. Ibid., p. 207.
34. Ibid., p. 212.
35. Bordwell defines compositional motivation as the justification of material 'in terms of its relevance to story necessity' (ibid., p. 36).
36. Barratt (2009), p. 67.
37. A close-up of the front of the Teddy Polaroid opens the second colour sequence. We then see the back of the image later in the sequence just prior to Leonard shooting Teddy and a third close-up of the back of the Polaroid begins the third colour sequence.
38. Bordwell (2008), pp. 79–80.
39. Enacted recounting is a convention, 'a character tells about past events, and the syuzhet presents the events in a flashback' (ibid., p. 78).
40. Transtextual relates in this instance to the expectation that certain generic codes will be present even if they are neither causally nor realistically necessary. See ibid., p. 36.
41. Arguably, given the primacy effect and the viewer identification with Leonard at this point in the narration, the second hypothesis is more likely during a second viewing.
42. Bordwell (2008), p. 64
43. External and internal flashbacks are those that occur outside the *syuzhet* or within the *syuzhet* respectively (ibid., p. 78).
44. Occurring around thirty-two minutes.
45. The narrational gaps at the end of the sequence are the omission of shot 2 and the shortening of shot 3 from colour sequence 8.
46. For instance, in the nineteen sequences from colour sequence 7–16 inclusive the narration presents duration in the following order: morning, day, evening, night, day, night, day, evening, day, dawn, morning, day, night, day, dawn, day, night, day, evening, night.
47. Branigan (1992), pp 176–9.

48. Murphy (2007), pp. 15–19.
49. Ibid., p. 16.
50. Hesmondhalgh (2008), p. 176.
51. Bordwell (2006), p. 75.
52. Ibid., p. 232.
53. Elsaesser (2009), p. 16.
54. 'Indie Angst', *New Times Los Angeles*, 15–21 March 2001, p. 17.

Chapter 4

1. Newmarket (2000) *Memento* Production Notes.
2. See *Memento* reviews in *Screen International*, 15 September 2000, p. 28; *Entertainment Today*, 16 March 2001; *Wall Street Journal*, 16 March 2001; *Village Voice*, 20 March 2001; *The Observer (London)*, 22 October 2000; *The Sunday Times*, 11 October 2000, p. 8; *GQ*, March 2001; *LA Weekly*, 23–29 March 2001, p. 37.
3. Neale (2000), p. 164.
4. Ibid.
5. Ibid., p. 165
6. Ibid.
7. Christopher Nolan, quoted in *New York Times*, 25 February 2001, p. 23.
8. Jameson (1993), pp. 74–7.
9. Naremore (2008), p. 211.
10. Ibid., p. 220.
11. Kaplan (1998), p. 9.
12. Chopra-Gant (2005), p. 26.
13. Hirsch (1999), p. 7.
14. Conard (2007b), p. 2.
15. Hirsch (1999), p. 10.
16. There are many excellent histories that chart the uses of the term *film noir* from 1946 and the establishment of a *noir* canon in the 1950s. For an account of the history of *noir* as an idea, see James Naremore, *More Than Night: Film Noir in its Contexts*, particularly chapter 1.
17. Hirsch (1999), p. 20.
18. Place (1998), p. 60.
19. Ibid.
20. Ibid., p. 58.
21. McDonnell (2007), p. 283.
22. For an extensive account of the rise of the New Man, see Nixon (1996).

23. Toerien and Durrheim (2001), p. 3.
24. Rose (2008), p. 50.
25. Shakespeare (1998), p. 150.

Chapter 5

1. Christopher Nolan, quoted in *New Times Los Angeles*, 15–21 March 2001, p. 14.
2. dr_gingivitis, New Jersey, 12 March 2001, *Memento* user comments at www.IMDb.com
3. David Ren, 18 March 2001, post #1 online at http://www.hometheaterforum.com/htf/movies-theatrical/5465-official-memento-discussion-thread.html (accessed 14 December 2008).
4. Chuck Schick, 20 March 2001, post #20, ibid.
5. See Ault, 3 April 2000, 'Hollywood.com', *Variety.com* http://www.variety.com/review/VE1117915543.html?categoryid=31&cs=1&query=IMDb+visitor [accessed 20 March 2009]; Terdiman, 16 March 2009, 'IMDb's Vision: Offer Streaming for Every Title', http://news.cnet.com/8301-1023_3-10197486-93.html (accessed 20 March 2009); Zarem, 9 July 2006, 'IMDb Media Network Case Study', http://www.mequoda.com/reviews-and-studies/publishing-case-studies/imdb-media-network-case-study/ (accessed 20 March 2009).
6. Brown, Broderick and Lee (2007), p. 3.
7. I refer here to the print advertisements for the film which appeared in *Los Angeles Times* in June 2001 and used the IMDb ranking list as the main image, with *Memento* at number 12 emboldened.
8. IMDb expires older posts from message boards so the discussion about *Memento* at the time of its release is no longer available. A sample of twenty archived message boards which contained more than five posts accessed from Google groups have also been used here, in addition to the IMDb user comments.
9. See Smith and Kollock (2003), p. 186.
10. Norris (2002), p. 4.
11. Bury (2003), p. 269.
12. The IMDb ratings system allows IMDb users to score films from 1 ('awful') to 10 ('excellent').
13. Figures here refer to percentages of the total male and total female populations. Internet usage is distinct from computer usage and all figures for usage cited are taken from the US Department of Commerce (2002) *A*

Nation Online based on the 2001 US Census Bureau's Current Population Survey available online at http://www.ntia.doc.gov/ntiahome/dn/html/toc.htm (accessed 10 July 2009).

14. Ibid.
15. Ibid.
16. Wyatt (1994), p. 96.
17. Bourdieu (1984), p. 173.
18. See Sarah Thornton's work on clubbing and subculture in Thornton (1995).
19. Jenkins (2006), p. 41.
20. Staiger (2005), p. 99.
21. Cosmo Landesman, 'One to Remember', *The Sunday Times*, 22 October 2000, p. 8.
22. Lee Marshall, '*Memento*', *Screen International*, 25 September 2000, p. 28.
23. Brent Simon, '*Memento*', *Entertainment Today*, 16 March 2001.
24. Joe Morgenstern, 'Hero with No Memory Turns "*Memento*" into Unforgettable Trip', *Wall Street Journal*, 16 March 2001.
25. James Mottram, 'Revenge is a Dish Best Served Backward,' *The Independent*, 15 October 2000.
26. Mark Das, 20 May 2001, '*Memento?*' posted at alt.movies newsgroup (accessed 21 December 2008).
27. Total user comments refers to the 1,500 comments used here and not the total number of comments posted.
28. Kenneth Bearden, '*Memento* Opinions', 3 April 2001, posted at alt.movies.independent (accessed 14 December 2008).
29. Posted at http://groups.google.com/group/alt.movies/browse_thread/thread/cc5a6231c8ee2bc4/2db0dc2849f0bacc? (accessed 14 December 2008).
30. Post #28, 17 September 2001, MovieForums.com at http://www.movieforums.com/community/showthread.php?t=857 (accessed 14 December 2008).
31. Oscar nominations were discussed in 6.1 per cent of the IMDb user comments.
32. Post #38, posted 13 February 2002, MovieForums, http://www.movieforums.com/community/showthread.php?t=1794 (accessed 14 December 2008).
33. See *Variety.com* online at http://www.variety.com/awardcentral_vstory/VR1117935961.html (accessed 29 July 2008).

Bibliography

Adelson, Andrea (1993) 'Advertising: For its Latest Golden Age, Radio Has Recast Itself to Advertisers as the Home of Niche Markets', *New York Times*, 28 December 1993 online http://query.nytimes.com/gst/fullpage.ht ml?res=9F0CE4DB1F3FF93BA15751C1A965958260 (accessed January 2009).

Barrett, Daniel (2009) '"Twist Blindness": The Role of Primacy, Priming, Schemas, and Recconstructive Memory in a First-Time Viewing of *The Sixth Sense*', in Warren Buckland (ed.) *Puzzle Film: Complex Storytelling in Contemporary Cinema*, Chichester: Wiley-Blackwell, pp. 62–86.

Berg, Charles Ramírez (2006) 'A Taxonomy of Alternative Plots in Recent Films: Classifying the "Tarantino Effect"', *Film Criticism*, Vol. XXXI, Nos. 1–2, Fall/Winter, pp. 5–61.

Berry, Glen (1999) 'The Internet as Equalizer', *MovieMaker*, October 1999, pp. 82–5.

Bing, Jonathan (2001) 'Cutting the Deck', *Filmmaker*, Winter 2001, Vol. 9, No. 2, p. 51.

Biskind, Peter (2007) *Down and Dirty Pictures: Miramax, Sundance and the Rise of Independent Film*, London: Bloomsbury.

Bordwell, David ([1985] 2008) *Narration in the Fiction Film*, London and New York: Routledge.

Bordwell, David (2006) *The Way Hollywood Tells It: Story and Style in Modern Movies*, Berkeley, Los Angeles and London University of California Press.

Bourdieu, Pierre (1984) *Distinction: A Social Critique of the Judgment of Taste*, Cambridge, MA: Harvard University Press.

Bourdieu, Pierre (1993) *The Field of Cultural Production*, Cambridge and Oxford: Polity.

Bowen, Peter (1995) 'The Little Rascals', *Filmmaker*, Summer 1995, online http://www.filmmakermagazine.com/summer1995/rascals.php (accessed 25 July 2008).

Branigan, Edward (1992) *Narrative Comprehension and Film*, London and New York: Routledge.

Broderick, Peter (1993) 'A Film for a Song', *Filmmaker*, online http://www.filmmakermagazine.com/winter1993/film_for_song.php (accessed 6 January 2009).

Brown, Jo, Broderick, Amanda J. and Lee, Nick (2007) 'Word of Mouth Communication with Online Communities: Conceptualizing the Online Social Network', *Journal of Interactive Marketing*, Vol. 21, No. 3, Summer, pp. 2–20.

Buckland, Warren (ed.) (2009) *Puzzle Film: Complex Storytelling in Contemporary Cinema*, Chichester: Wiley-Blackwell.

Bury, Rhiannon (2003) '"The X-Files", Online Fan Culture, and the David Duchovny Estrogen Brigades', in David Muggleton and Rupert Weinzierl (eds) *The Post-Subcultures Reader*, Oxford and New York: Berg.

Carver, Benedict (1999) 'Newmarket Bows Video Distribution Arm', *Variety*, 9 July, pp. 1 and 26.

Chatman, Seymour (1980) *Story and Discourse: Narrative Structure in Fiction and Film*, Ithaca NY and London: Cornell University Press.

Chopra-Gant, Mike (2005) *Hollywood Genres and Postwar America: Masculinity, Family and Nation in Popular Movies and Film Noir*, London and New York: I. B. Tauris.

Conard, Mark T. (ed.) (2007a) *The Philosophy of Film Noir*, Kentucky: The University Press of Kentucky.

Conard, Mark T. (ed.) (2007b) *The Philosophy of Neo-Noir*, Kentucky: The University Press of Kentucky.

Corliss, Richard and Elizabeth Bland (1993) 'Don't Read This Story', *Time Magazine*, 1 March 1993, online http://www.time.com/time/magazine/article/0,9171,977831,00.html (accessed 8 December 2008).

Corliss, Richard and Georgia Harbison (1993) 'Few Bucks, Very Big Bang', *Time Magazine*, 8 March 1993, online http://www.time.com/time/magazine/article/0,9171,977898,00.html (accessed 8 December 2008).

Diorio, Carl (2001) 'Indie Pix Cash Pool Drying Up', *Variety.com* 26 April 2001, online http://www.variety.com/index.asp?layout=print_story&articleid=VR1117797910&categoryid=13 (accessed 29 July 2008).

Elsaesser, Thomas (2009) 'The Mind-Game Film', in Warren Buckland (ed.) *Puzzle Film: Complex Storytelling in Contemporary Cinema*, Chichester: Wiley-Blackwell, pp. 13–41.

Filmmaker Magazine (1996) 'The Fifty Most Important Independent Films', *Filmmaker Magazine: The Magazine of Independent Film*, Fall, Vol. 5, No. 1, pp. 40–60.

Goodridge, Mike (1998) 'Artisan Reaches for Summit', *Screen International*, 17 April 1998.

Goodridge, Mike (2004) 'Newmarket in the Limelight', *Screen International*, 7 May 2004, p. 10.

Green, Jay (1994a) 'Battered, but Still Standing', *Variety.com*, 25 February 1994, online http://www.variety.com/index.asp?layout=print_story&articleid=VR118621&categoryid=18 (accessed 29 July 2008).

Green, Jay (1994b) 'Ex-Daiwa exex Open Loan Biz', *Variety.com*, 3 March 1994, online http://www.variety.com/article/VR118829.html?categoryid=18&cs=1 (accessed 28 July 2008).

Grove, Christopher (1998) 'Newmarket Group Mints Money for Mid-Budget Pix', *Variety*, 5 November 1998, pp. A4 and A12.

Groves, Don (1993) 'Guiness, CBC Launch Film Fund', *Variety.com*, 12 February 1993, online http://www.variety.com/article/VR103897.html?categoryid=18&cs=1 (accessed 28 July 2008).

Harris, Dana and Charles Lyons (2002) 'Indie Distrib Whiz Joining Newmarket', *Variety*, 24 July 2002 pp. 1 and 38.

Hesmondhalgh, David (2008) *The Cultural Industries*, 2nd edition, Los Angeles and London: Sage.

Hillier, Jim (ed.) ([2001] 2006) *American Independent Cinema*, London: BFI Publishing.

Hirsch, Foster (1999) *Detours and Lost Highways: A Map of Neo-Noir*, New York: Limelight Editions.

Hollywood Reporter (2001) 'Memento Doubles its Theater Take' *Hollywood Reporter*, 25 October 2001.

Hollywood Reporter (2008) 'Indie Power 50', *Hollywood Reporter*, 17 January 2008.

Holmlund, Chris and Justin Wyatt (2005) *Contemporary American Independent Film: From the Margins to the Mainstream*, London and New York: Routledge.

Jameson, Fredric (1993) 'Postmodernism, or The Cultural Logic of Late Capitalism' in Thomas Docherty, *Postmodernism: A Reader*, Hemel Hempstead: Harvester Wheatsheaf, pp. 62–92.

Jenkins, Henry (1992) *Textual Poachers: Television Fans and Participatory Culture*, New York: Routledge.

Jenkins, Henry (2006) *Fans, Bloggers and Gamers: Exploring Participatory Culture*, New York: New York University Press.

Kaplan, E. Ann (ed.) (1998) *Women In Film Noir*, London: BFI Publishing.

King, Geoff (2005) *American Independent Cinema*, London and New York: I.B. Tauris.

King, Geoff (2007) *New Hollywood Cinema: An Introduction*, London and New York: I.B. Tauris.

Kleinhans, Chuck (1998) 'Independent Features: Hopes and Dreams', in Jon Lewis (ed.) (1998) *The New American Cinema*, Durham, NC and London, Duke University Press, pp. 307–27.

Kotler, Steven (2006) 'Mavericks to Mainstreamers: Indie's Rebel Helmers Have Morphed into Hollywood's Megapic Maestros', *Vairety.com*, 11 January, online http://www.variety.com/awardcentral_vstory/VR1117935961. html (accessed 3 August 2009).

Kunz, William (2007) *Culture Conglomerates: Consolidation in the Motion Picture and Television Industries*, Oxford: Rowan & Littlefield.

Levy, Emmanuel (1999) *Cinema of Outsiders: The Rise of American Independent Film*, New York and London: New York University Press.

Lewis, Jon (ed.) (1998) *The New American Cinema*, Durham, NC and London, Duke University Press.

Lucia, Cynthia and Porton, Richard (1999) 'Editorial', *Cineaste*, Vol. XXIV, No. 4, p. 1.

Lyons, Donald (1994) *Independent Visions: A Critical Introduction to Recent Independent American Film*, New York: Ballantine Books.

Martesko, Karol (1996) 'Letter from the Publisher', *Filmmaker Magazine: The Magazine of Independent Film*, Fall, Vol. 5, No. 1, p. 4.

McDonnell, Brian (2007) 'Memento', in Geoff Mayer and Brian McDonnell, *Encyclopedia of Film Noir*, Westport, CT: Greenwood Press.

Mitchell, Elvis (2003) 'Cannes Film Festival: Trading War Stories in Cannes' Doldrums', *The New York Times*, 22 May 2003, online http://query.nytimes. com/gst/fullpage.html?res=9E07EFDA1E3EF931A15756C0A9659C8B 63&sec=&spon=&pagewanted=2 (accessed 10 December 2008).

Mittell, Jason (2006) 'Narrative Complexity in Contemporary American Television', *The Velvet Light Trap*, Fall, No. 58, pp. 29–40.

Moran, Jim and Willis, Holly (1998) 'The War of Independents', *Filmmaker: The Magazine of Independent Film*, Winter, Vol. 6, No. 2, p. 22.

Mottram, James (2005) *The Making of Memento*, New York: Faber and Faber.

Mottram, James (2006) *The Sundance Kids: How the Mavericks Took Back Hollywood*, New York: Faber and Faber.

MovieMaker (1994) '*Clerks* Proves Ignorance is Bliss', *MovieMaker*, 1 October 1994, online http://www.moviemaker.com/directing/article/kevin_smith_ clerks_scott_mosier_20080908/ (accessed 24 July 2008).

Murphy, J. J. (2007) *Me and You and Memento and Fargo: How Independent Screenplays Work*, New York and London, Continuum.

Nancarrow, Clive, Pamela Nancarrow and Julie Page (2001) 'An Analysis of the Concept of *Cool* and its Marketing Implications', *Journal of Consumer Behaviour*, Vol. 1, No. 4, pp. 311–22.

Naremore, James (2008) *More Than Night: Film Noir in its Contexts*, Los Angeles and London: University of California Press.

Neale, Steve (2000) *Genre and Hollywood*, London and New York: Routledge.

Nelson, Randy and Atchison, Doug (2003) 'The Economics of the Oscars', *MovieMaker*, 7 January 2003, online https://www.moviemaker.com/directing/article/the_economics_of_oscar_3011/ (accessed 24 July 2008).

Newman, Michael Z. (2006) 'Character and Complexity in American Independent Cinema: *21 Grams* and *Passion Fish*', *Film Criticism*, Fall/Winter, Vol. XXXI, Nos. 1–2, pp. 89–106.

Nixon, Sean (1996) *Hard Looks: Masculinities, Spectatorship and Contemporary Consumption*, New York: St. Martin's Press.

Nolan, Christopher (2001) *Memento & Following*, London and New York: Faber and Faber.

Norris, Pippa (2002) 'The Bridging and Bonding Role of Online Communities', *The Harvard International Journal of Press/Politics*, Volume 7, No. 3, pp. 3–13.

Panek, Elliot (2006) 'The Poet and the Detective: Defining the Psychological Puzzle Film', *Film Criticism*, Fall/Winter, Vol. XXXI, Nos. 1–2, pp. 62–88.

Place, Janey (1998) 'Women in Film Noir', in E. Ann Kaplan (ed.), *Women in Film Noir*, London: BFI Publishing, pp. 47–68.

Rhys, Timothy (2003) 'Why Independent Film is Alive and Well', *MovieMaker*, 2 May 2003, online http://www.moviemaker.com/directing/article/why_independent_film_is_alive_and_well_3264/ (accessed 10 December 2008).

Rose, Irene (2008) 'Popular Fiction and Representations of Disability', *Popular Narrative Media*, Spring, Vol. 1, Issue 1, pp. 43–58.

Seguin, Denis (2001) 'Fest Victors Struggle to Find US Distribs', *Screen International*, 27 April 2001, pp. 1 and 14.

Shakespeare, Tom (1998) *The Disability Studies Reader: Social Science Perspectives*, London: Continuum.

Smith, Marc and Kollock, Peter (2003) *Communities in Cyberspace*, London and New York: Routledge.

Staiger, Janet (2005) *Media Reception Studies*, New York and London: New York University Press.

Staiger, Janet (2006) 'Complex Narratives, an Introduction' *Film Criticism*, Fall/Winter, Vol. XXXI, Nos. 1–2, pp. 2–4.

Tarantino, Quentin (1994) 'Quentin Tarantino on "Pulp Fiction"', *Sight and Sound*, May, Vol. 4, Issue 5, pp. 10–11.

Thompson, Kristin (1999) *Storytelling in the New Hollywood: Understanding Classical Narrative Technique*, Cambridge, MA and London: Harvard University Press.

Thornton, Sarah (1995) *Club Cultures: Music, Media and Subcultural Capital*, Cambridge: Polity.

Toerien, Merran and Durrheim, Kevin (2001) 'Power Through Knowledge: Ignorance and the "Real Man"', *Feminism & Psychology*, Vol. 11, No. 1, pp. 35–54.

Tzioumakis, Yannis (2006a) *American Independent Cinema: An Introduction*, Edinburgh: Edinburgh University Press.

Tzioumakis, Yannis (2006b) 'Marketing David Mamet: Institutionally Assigned Film Authorship and Contemporary American Cinema', *The Velvet Light Trap*, Spring, No. 57, pp. 60–75.

Tzioumakis, Yannis (2009) *The Spanish Prisoner*, Edinburgh: Edinburgh University Press.

Wallace, Amy (1999) 'Behind the "Witch"', *Los Angeles Times*, 26 July 1999, pp. F1 and F11.

Wallace, Amy (2000) 'No Fame Please, Just Go See Our Pictures', *Los Angeles Times*, 19 May 2000, pp. F2 and F17.

West, Joan. M. and West, Dennis (1999) 'Not Playing by the Usual Rules: An Interview with John Sayles', *Cineaste*, Vol. XXIV, No. 4, pp. 28–31.

Wyatt, Justin (1994) *High Concept: Movies and Marketing in Hollywood*, Austin, TX: University of Texas Press.

Wyatt, Justin (1998) 'The Formation of the "Major Independent"' in S. Neale and M. Smith (eds) *Contemporary Hollywood Cinema*, London: Routledge, pp. 74–90.

Wyatt, Justin (2005) '1970s Distribution and Marketing Strategies' in Christine Holmlund and Justin Wyatt, *Contemporary American Independent Film: From the Margins to the Mainstream*, London: Routledge, pp. 229–244.

Index